Pair Programming with ChatGPT

AI-Enhanced Coding for the Modern Developer (Covers ChatGPT 4)

Michael D. Callaghan

Copyright © 2023 Michael D. Callaghan

All rights reserved.

No part of this book may be reproduced, stored in a retrieval system, or transmitted in any form or by any means, electronic, mechanical, photocopying, recording, or otherwise, without the prior written permission of the publisher, except for brief quotations used in critical articles and reviews.

Requests for permission to reproduce material from this book should be directed to michael@walkingriver.com.

This book is sold subject to the condition that it shall not, by way of trade or otherwise, be lent, resold, hired out, or otherwise circulated without the publisher's prior consent in any form of binding or cover other than that in which it is published and without a similar condition, including this condition, being imposed on the subsequent purchaser.

While every effort has been made to ensure the accuracy of the information contained in this book, the author and publisher make no representations or warranties, express or implied, about the completeness, accuracy, reliability, suitability or availability with respect to the information, products, services, or related graphics contained in the book for any purpose. Any reliance you place on such information is therefore strictly at your own risk.

In no event will the author or publisher be liable for any loss or damage including without limitation, indirect or consequential loss or damage, or any loss or damage whatsoever arising from loss of data or profits arising out of, or in connection with, the use of this book.

If you find any errors or inaccuracies, please contact the publisher.

Cover design by Michael D. Callaghan

CONTENTS

Title Page
Copyright
Preface
Using AI in Software Development   1
Shell Scripting Commands   13
Common Algorithms   34
Learning RxJS   53
Angular's HttpClient   65
Regular Expressions   82
Data Generation   103
Agile Project Management   128
Let's Build an App!   142
Unit Testing   151
Other Considerations   167
The Future of Software Development   194
Books By This Author   199
Pair Programming   201
About The Author   203

PREFACE

About This Book

This book is designed to be a fun, easy-to-read, and hands-on exploration of using Artificial Intelligence tools as your "pair programming" partner. Throughout the book, I hope you'll see how you can use ChatGPT to make your own tasks easier and more effective.

Over the length of the book, we'll cover the following topics:

- Using AI in Software Development
- Shell Scripting Commands
- Common Algorithms
- Learning RxJS
- Angular's HttpClient
- Regular Expressions
- Data Generation
- Agile Project Management
- Let's Build an App!
- Unit Testing
- Other Considerations
- The Future of Software Development

My goal is to inspire you to come up with your own ideas and vastly improve your efficiency.

Who is This Book For?

This book is for any software developer of any level, from "just starting out" to "ready to retire." Though most of my examples use specific web technologies like HTML, JavaScript, TypeScript, and Ionic, you don't need to be familiar with these languages and frameworks to get something out of this book.

Following Along

Regardless of the type of software development you do, I'm sure you'll find value by following along in whatever language you prefer.

I'm pleased to offer you a list of most of the prompts I use throughout the book, in case you want to follow along and don't want to type them. You can sign up and download them free of charge here:

https://walkingriver.gumroad.com/l/pair-programming-bonus

Those who sign up for my bonus materials will also be eligible for occasional sneak peeks and discounts on future books and other content.

Updates and Questions

If you ever have questions or just want to be updated about this and future books, feel free to sign up at the link above, or send an email to michael@walkingriver.com.

I'm also very active on Twitter, where you can find me posting as @WalkingRiver.

Books on Amazon

You can find the rest of my titles on Amazon at https://amazon.com/author/mcallaghan.

If you enjoy this book, I'd appreciate you leaving me a positive review on Amazon, which you can do here: https://www.amazon.com/review/create-review?asin=B0C56TTL2V

USING AI IN SOFTWARE DEVELOPMENT

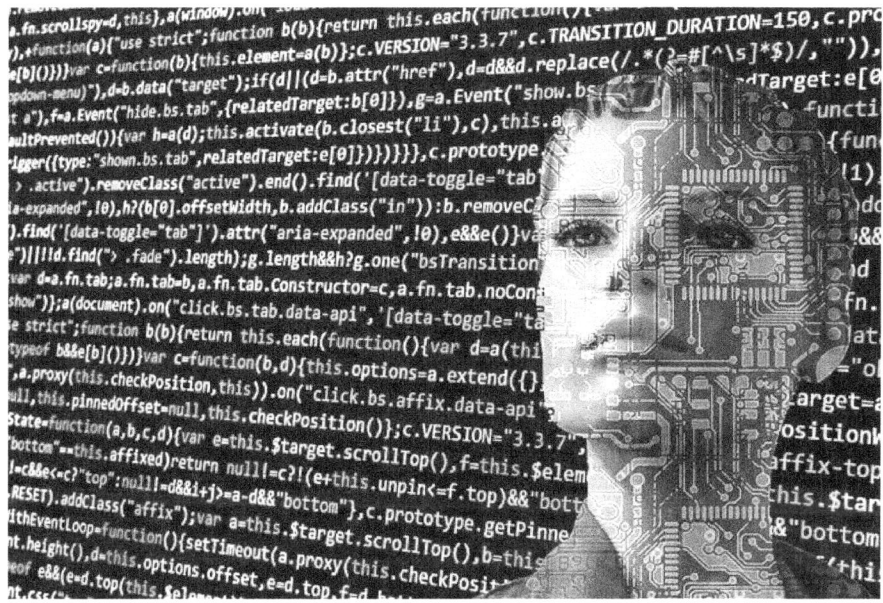

Image by Gerd Altmann on Pixabay

I first heard about using AI for programming with the introduction of GitHub Copilot in mid-2022. I was intrigued by the idea that someone trained an Artificial Intelligence (henceforth "AI") model from the source code inside every public GitHub repo. Further, that once the model had been trained, it could essentially understand my source code and make suggestions in real time. If this were real, I had to try it.

I registered for the free beta and waited. About a week later, I got the email accepting me into the beta program, along with a link to install a Visual Studio Code extension. I installed the extension and started playing with it. It seemed cool but I don't do a lot of day-to-day coding on my personal machine and wasn't ready to install Beta software on my work computer. So, I promptly forgot about it for a while.

Fast forward a few months. ChatGPT showed up and took the world by storm. Here was the first "approachable" AI with a conversational interface. People could ask it questions and expect a coherent answer.

Millions of people began experimenting with it, seeing how well it could write code simply by entering a brief description of the problem. While not perfect, its answers were surprisingly good. People began wondering whether we had entered a strange new world of software development, one where traditional coding, and software developers, would soon be obsolete.

What We Will Cover

My objective in writing this book is to describe how AI can be used in the day-to-day activities of a typical software developer. Before we dive deep into these concepts, let's take a high-level look at what the tools can and cannot do for us.

What Can AI Tools Do?

1. Code generation: AI can be used to generate code based on a set of inputs and requirements, which can speed up the

development process and reduce the chance of errors.
2. Test automation: AI can be used to automatically generate test cases and test scripts, which can save time and improve the quality of software.
3. Quality assurance: AI can be used to automatically evaluate the quality of code, which can help identify potential issues before they become problems.
4. UI/UX design: AI can be used to generate UI/UX designs, which can save time and improve the overall user experience.
5. Language Processing: AI can be used for natural language processing, which can be used in natural language interface for software development.
6. Predictive analytics: AI can be used to predict future trends, bugs and areas that need attention.
7. AI-powered search: AI can be used to search and recommend relevant code snippets, libraries and tools to developers.

I will be focusing on the first two items in that list, as they seem most relevant to software development today.

What are Their Limitations?

1. Limited understanding of context: AI may not fully understand the context in which code is being written, which can lead to

errors or inconsistencies.
2. Lack of creativity: AI can generate code or designs that are functional but may lack the creativity of a human developer.
3. Limited ability to handle complexity: AI may struggle with complex code or designs that involve many variables and interdependencies.
4. Lack of understanding of industry standards and best practices: AI may not be aware of the best practices and standards in a particular industry or field, which can lead to suboptimal results.
5. Lack of flexibility: AI may not be able to adapt to changing requirements or unexpected situations as well as a human developer.
6. Limited ability to handle unstructured data: AI may struggle with data that is not well-organized or does not conform to a specific format.
7. Limited ability to generalize: AI may struggle to generalize from examples and may not work well in situations where it has not been explicitly trained.
8. Data bias: AI models can perpetuate human biases if the training data is not diverse and representative of the population.
9. Dependence on large amounts of data: AI models often require large amounts of data to be trained, which can be difficult to

acquire and process.
10. Lack of explainability: AI models can be opaque, making it difficult to understand how they arrived at a particular decision or output. As we will see, this is where ChatGPT shines.

What is Covered in This Book

There are a lot of AI tools that we could choose. I won't pretend to know even half of them. The two with the biggest market penetration and clout seem to be ChatGPT from OpenAI and Copilot from GitHub. I will focus on ChatGPT-4 throughout the book.

You can check out my other titles to see similar discussions of other tools.

ChatGPT

ChatGPT is a language model developed by OpenAI. It is a variant of the GPT (Generative Pre-trained Transformer) model, which is trained on a massive amount of internet text data to generate human-like text. The model is fine-tuned for specific tasks, such as language translation, text summarization, and conversation. With its ability to understand and respond to natural language inputs, ChatGPT can be used for a variety of applications, such as chatbots, virtual assistants, and language-based games.

People discovered very quickly that it can also be used to generate functioning computer code in a variety of languages. ChatGPT, as a powerful language generation model, can be used in several ways to help with software development:

1. Code generation: ChatGPT can be used to generate code snippets and even complete functions based on a set of inputs and requirements, which can speed up the development process and reduce the chance of errors.
2. Text generation: ChatGPT can be used to generate comments, documentation and even commit messages, which can save developers time and improve code readability.
3. Test case generation: ChatGPT can be used to generate test cases and test scripts for software, which can save time and improve the quality of software.

To use ChatGPT, you will need to sign up for an OpenAI API account, which you can do at https://chat.openai.com/chat. If you already have an account with OpenAI, you can log in with that. If not, you will need to register.

At the time of this writing, there are two tiers to the service: one is free, but you may find that it is frequently "at capacity," which makes it hard to use.

There is also a paid tier, ChatGPT PLUS, which is currently $20 USD per month. OpenAI has also announced plans for additional tiers, as well as a waitlist so you can get more information.

This book will cover GPT-4, which requires a PLUS subscription.

How does it Compare to Tools Like Copilot?

ChatGPT and GitHub Copilot are both AI-powered tools that are designed to assist software developers in their work. Both tools use machine learning algorithms to provide developers with intelligent suggestions and assistance, but they are designed for different aspects of the development process.

One of the main differences between the two tools is their area of focus. ChatGPT is focused on natural language processing tasks, while GitHub Copilot is focused on code completion and suggestions. ChatGPT can be used to generate text responses or code, while GitHub Copilot can be used primarily to generate code snippets.

Another difference is the way the two tools are used. ChatGPT is accessed through a chat-like interface (hence the name), so developers tend to be more descriptive in using it to generate code. On the other hand, GitHub Copilot is integrated into the development environment and can be used directly inside your project.

Controversy - Should Developers Use These Tools?

I thought I should get this out of the way early because there are those who feel the answer is a definite "no."

One of the main concerns regarding ChatGPT's training on a broad dataset from the internet is that it may propagate poor coding habits and security vulnerabilities. Since ChatGPT learns from a diverse range of sources, it might inadvertently pick up and promote suboptimal coding practices or security risks that exist in its training data. This could potentially lead developers to inadvertently incorporate these practices into their own code, possibly leading to security breaches or other complications.

Another potential risk is that developers might become overly reliant on ChatGPT's suggestions, thereby diminishing the significance of their own understanding of the codebase. This dependency could deter developers from acquiring an in-depth knowledge of the code they're working with, making it more challenging to maintain and troubleshoot issues in the future.

Moreover, even though OpenAI claims to use certain privacy techniques to protect the individuality of training data and ensure that ChatGPT doesn't remember specific documents, concerns about privacy and data security can arise. While ChatGPT is not designed to recall or generate sensitive data like usernames, passwords, or other personal information, there is always a risk that the AI could unintentionally generate such information if it were present in the training data.

Licensing Issues

One of the larger criticisms and causes of the controversy stem from licensing issues with the data used to train the AI models. This can be a significant concern, as using code without proper permission or licensing can lead to legal issues. Some specific issues that can arise include:

1. Copyright infringement if the data used to train an AI model is protected by copyright.
2. Trade secret infringement if the data used to train an AI model constitutes someone else's trade secret.
3. If the data used to train an AI model contains personal information, using it without proper permission or anonymizing it may violate privacy laws.
4. If the data used to train an AI model is subject to a license or contract, using it in a way that violates those terms can lead to legal issues.

It's important for developers and organizations to be aware of these issues and to obtain proper permissions and licenses for any data used to train AI models. This can include obtaining licenses for open-source datasets or negotiating agreements with data providers to use proprietary data.

No Respecter of Licenses

When using AI to help write software, it is important to consider the open-source licenses of the code that may have been used to train the AI. Open-source licenses are agreements that dictate how the code covered by the license can be used, modified, and distributed. Different open-source licenses have different terms and conditions, so it is important to carefully review the licenses of any code that is used to train the AI and ensure that they are being complied with. This may involve obtaining the proper permissions, giving credit to the original authors, and making any required changes to the code. Failing to properly comply with open-source licenses can result in legal consequences, such as being sued for copyright infringement.

A concrete example may illustrate the issue more clearly. In one of my mobile apps, I use an algorithm I found to generate a deck of cards of an arbitrary size. The JavaScript code I found on GitHub (not using any AI) is clearly marked as "GPL Licensed." As I understand it (and I'm not a lawyer), this means that I am free to use this algorithm in my own code, and can even sell the app. That's allowed. However, I must include the GPL notice in the source code. I must also release my source code under the same license.

What if I had used an AI that suggested this algorithm to me and I was unaware of its license, and then proceeded to offer my app under a different license? Would I technically be in violation of the GPL from the original algorithm? If so, what risk would this expose me or my employer to? Unfortunately, these types of questions will probably need to be settled in courts. As I write this, there is at least one lawsuit pending regarding GitHub Copilot's use of licensed software in its recommendations. I am not currently aware of any such lawsuits against OpenAI, but there very well could be.

Ethical Considerations

What are the ethics of using AI to help with software development? Is it ethical to use an AI to help write software? Can the developer or company really claim that they are the proper authors of said software? This may seem odd, but I asked ChatGPT that very question. This is how it replied.

> It is generally considered ethical to use AI to assist in the development of software, as long as the developers and the company are transparent about the role of the AI in the development process and give credit where it is due. The developer or company can claim authorship of the software but should also acknowledge the contributions of the AI used in the development process. Additionally, it is important to ensure that any AI models used in the development of software are trained on ethically sourced data and do not perpetuate any biases.

I also asked it whether there are any other ethical considerations to be aware of.

> First, there is the issue of fairness and bias. It is important to ensure that the AI system is not making decisions based on biased data, as this could result in unfair treatment of certain individuals or groups. Additionally, there is the question of accountability. It is important to consider who is responsible for any errors or mistakes made by the AI system, and to ensure that there are appropriate safeguards in place to prevent such errors from happening. Finally, there is the issue of privacy. It is important to ensure that the personal data of users is collected, used, and stored in a manner that respects their privacy and complies with relevant laws and regulations.

Conventions Used in This Book

As you see above, I am adopting the convention of printing the output from the AI in a different font and background, so that you can easily see distinguish my thoughts from the AI's.

> When I show a prompt to ChatGPT, I will show it like this.

> Output used verbatim from ChatGPT will be shown this way.

```
Also, any commands or generated source code will be shown this way.
```

SHELL SCRIPTING COMMANDS

Image by cocoandwifi from Pixabay

Shell scripting is a fundamental skill for anyone who wants to efficiently manage and automate tasks on a computer.

Let's investigate how ChatGPT does with shell scripting. A while back I wrote an article about what these symbols (~|&||&&$!`()?) mean in a bash (or similar) shell and how to use them. Can ChatGPT give me these types of commands from nothing but comments? Read on to find out.

ChatGPT is ideally suited for these sorts of things, given its conversational nature. Here is how it responded to my first prompt:

> Check for a directory and print a message if it doesn't exist
>
> You can use the **test** command (also known as [or [[) to check if a directory exists, and the **echo** command to print a message if it doesn't. Here is an example:
>
> ```
> if test ! -d /path/to/directory; then
>         echo "Directory does not exist"
> fi
> ```
>
> Alternatively, you could use the **if [! -d "/path/to/directory"]; then** command with the same echo message.
>
> Another option is to use if [[! -d "/path/to/directory"]]; then

As you can see, ChatGPT offers an explanation with its answers and does not simply give you the code. As you will see, this can be a significant advantage to using ChatGPT.

The find Command

The next thing I tried was to find all the PDF files anywhere in my home directory and below. Normally when I do that, I use the find command. Is that what ChatGPT would suggest? I entered the following comment, which led to two different options.

> Find all PDF files in my home directory and print the path to each one
>
> You can use the **find** command to search for all PDF files in your home directory and print the path to each one. Here's an example:

```
find ~ -name "*.pdf" -print
```

This will search for all files in your home directory (~) that end in **.pdf** and print the path to each one.

Alternatively, you could use **ls** command with wildcard,

```
ls ~/ -R | grep .pdf$
```

This will recursively list all files in your home directory, and filter only the files with .pdf extension.

As before, I appreciate that it provides an explanation and not just the command. If you are trying to learn, this is the better experience.

Background Tasks

The next thing I wanted to do was to determine whether the AI knows how to use some of those symbols that often trip up beginners. Would they know that the greater than sign (>) is used to redirect output and that the ampersand (&) is used to run a command in the background?

I changed my comment as follows, and then gave it the same hint from above. As before, ChatGPT gave me multiple options, complete with thorough explanations.

Find all PDF files below my home folder and write the results to a file called pdfs.txt in the background.

You can use the **find** command to search for all PDF files below your home directory, and the **tee** command to write the results to a file called pdfs.txt in the background. Here's an example:

```
find ~ -name "*.pdf" -print | tee pdfs.txt &
```

This will search for all files in your home directory and its

15

subdirectories that end in **.pdf** and print the path to each one. The output will be piped to the **tee** command, which will write it to a file called pdfs.txt in the current directory. The **&** at the end will run the command in background, so you can continue to use the terminal.

Alternatively, you could use **ls** command with wildcard,

```
ls ~/ -R | grep .pdf$ >> pdfs.txt &
```

This will recursively list all files in your home directory and its subdirectories, and filter only the files with .pdf extension, and write it to pdfs.txt file. The **&** at the end will run the command in background as well.

I had forgotten all about the `tee` command. I'm also impressed that it went a little farther with the `ls` command, using `grep` with a simple regular expression to find files that end in `.pdf`. It also assumed I would want to append to my `pdfs.txt` file if it already exists. Though not exactly what I asked for, it actually gave me more.

Output Pipe

Next, I wanted to see whether its know how to use the output of one command as the input to another.

Count the number of PDF files in my home folder in the background and print the result.

To count the number of PDF files in your home folder in the background and print the result, you can use the find command along with the wc command. Here's the command you can use in your zsh shell:

```
find ~/ -iname "*.pdf" -type f | wc -l &
```

Let's break down the command:

> find ~/ -iname "*.pdf": This command searches for files with the extension .pdf in your home directory (~). The -iname option is used to make the search case-insensitive.
>
> -type f is used to limit the search to only regular files (excluding directories or other types of files).
>
> |: This is a pipe symbol that redirects the output of the find command to the input of the next command.
>
> wc -l: This command counts the number of lines in its input. By using the -l option, it counts the number of lines, which in this case corresponds to the number of PDF files found.
>
> &: This ampersand symbol runs the command in the background.
>
> After executing the command, it will print the number of PDF files found in your home folder. The command will continue running in the background, allowing you to continue using the shell.

Redirect Errors to Ignore Them

Most people know how to use the > character to redirect the output of a command to a file. If the command encounters any errors, those will still display in the terminal, which can be confusing when running the command in the background.

I know it is possible to redirect errors to a special file called **/dev/null**, so that they are ignored completely. Unfortunately, I can never remember the syntax. I don't know why because it isn't that complicated. It's one of my weird blind spots, I suppose.

What's really cool about ChatGPT is that it remembers earlier parts of your conversation. For this one, I changed up the prompt and simply asked it to "rewrite the last command to ignore any errors." The explanation itself is also context-aware.

> Rewrite the last command to ignore any errors
>
> Certainly! To ignore any errors that may occur during the execution of the command and still count the number of PDF files in your home folder, you can use the following modified command:
>
> find ~/ -iname "*.pdf" -type f 2>/dev/null | wc -l &
>
> In this command, we've added 2>/dev/null to redirect the error output (file not found errors, permission denied errors, etc.) to the null device /dev/null, effectively discarding them.
>
> With this modification, any errors that occur during the execution of the find command will be suppressed, and only the count of PDF files will be printed. The command will continue running in the background.

*nix System Administration

I started wondering whether ChatGPT could help me with some common system administration tasks, such as creating users, adding users to groups, and so forth.

Add a New User Account

I decided to start with something simple, so I asked it to create a new user account for me.

ChatGPT again outdid itself, providing plenty of detail and explanation.

> Create a new user account on macos
>
> To create a new user account on macOS, you can use the dscl (Directory Service command line utility) command. Here is an

example of how to create a new user account called "newuser" with a password of "newpassword":

```
sudo dscl . -create /Users/newuser
sudo dscl . -create /Users/newuser UserShell /bin/bash
sudo dscl . -create /Users/newuser RealName "New User"
sudo dscl . -create /Users/newuser UniqueID "501"
sudo dscl . -create /Users/newuser PrimaryGroupID 20
sudo dscl . -create /Users/newuser NFSHomeDirectory /Users/newuser
sudo dscl . -passwd /Users/newuser newpassword
```

This creates the account, sets the shell to /bin/bash, sets the RealName, UniqueID, PrimaryGroupID and home directory, and sets the password.

Alternatively, you can use the **sysadminctl** command to create a new user account and set the password. Here is an example:

```
sudo sysadminctl -addUser newuser -fullName "New User" -password newpassword -admin
```

This creates the account with the username "newuser", full name "New User", password "newpassword" and admin privilege.

You also can use the GUI by going to System Preferences > Users & Groups > click on the lock icon to unlock it > click on the "+" sign to add a new user.

Please note that these commands require administrative privileges and should be used with caution.

I tried the second command on my Mac and it worked flawlessly.

Make an Existing User an Admin

Next, I asked for the command to make an existing user an admin. ChatGPT gave me a set of options.

> Make user 'michael' a local administrator
>
> To make a user "michael" a local administrator on macOS, you can use the **dscl** (Directory Service command line utility) command. Here is an example of how to make the user "michael" a local administrator:
>
> ```
> sudo dscl . -append /Groups/admin GroupMembership michael
> ```
>
> This command adds the user "michael" to the "admin" group. Members of the "admin" group have administrative privileges on the system.
>
> Alternatively, you can use the **dseditgroup** command to add a user to the "admin" group. Here is an example:
>
> ```
> sudo dseditgroup -o edit -a michael -t user admin
> ```
>
> This command adds the user "michael" to the "admin" group.
>
> You also can use the GUI by going to System Preferences > Users & Groups > click on the lock icon to unlock it > right click on the user you want to change > select "Advanced Options" > change the "Account type" to "Administrator".
>
> Please note that these commands require administrative privileges and should be used with caution.

Backup Files

Have you ever used `rsync` to back up files from one system to another? No? Of course not. No one does (ok, maybe some people do). It's hard to remember the syntax. That's why Dropbox and other such services exist.

ChatGPT gave me four different suggestions, with `rsync` being the first one. It also suggested using `scp`, which I had planned to ask about next.

> Sync my home folder to a remote server
>
> There are several ways to sync your home folder to a remote server on macOS. Here are a few options:
>
> **rsync**: This command-line tool can be used to synchronize files and directories between two locations. Here's an example of how to use **rsync** to sync your home folder to a remote server:
>
> ```
> rsync -avz -e ssh ~/ username@remote-server:/path/to/remote/folder/
> ```
>
> This command will sync all files and directories in your home folder to the specified remote server. The **-a** option tells **rsync** to preserve file permissions and ownership, the **-v** option provides verbose output, and the **-z** option enables compression to speed up the transfer. The **-e** option specifies the remote shell to use, in this case **ssh**.
>
> **scp**: This command-line tool can be used to copy files and directories between a local machine and a remote server. Here's an example of how to use **scp** to sync your home folder to a remote server:
>
> ```
> scp -r ~/ username@remote-server:/path/to/remote/folder/
> ```
>
> This command will copy all files and directories in your home folder to the specified remote server. The **-r** option tells **scp** to copy directories recursively.
>
> Finder: You also can use Finder to sync your home folder to a remote server by mounting the remote folder as a local volume using SMB, NFS or FTP protocols, and then use the Finder to copy the files and folders.
>
> Third party software: There are also third-party software like ChronoSync, Carbon Copy Cloner, and others that can be used to sync your home folder to a remote server.

Please note that these commands require a remote server with the appropriate permissions and access to be set up, and also make sure you have the correct login credentials to access the remote server.

Securely Copy from Server to Local

Instead of backing up files, maybe there are some files on a remote server that you want to copy locally. You might use a command like this. ChatGPT had already suggested `scp` as one possible method to synchronize files to a remote server, and I fully expected it to get this one with ease.

Securely Copy from Server to Local folder

To securely copy files from a remote server to a local folder on macOS, you can use the **scp** command. **scp** stands for "secure copy" and it uses the SSH protocol to transfer files.

Here's an example of how to use **scp** to copy a file called "file.txt" from the remote server "remote-server" to the local folder "~/Downloads":

```
scp username@remote-server:/path/to/file.txt ~/Downloads
```

This command will copy the file "file.txt" from the specified path on the remote server to the "Downloads" folder in your home directory.

You can also copy a directory and its contents by adding the -r option, which stands for "recursive"

```
scp -r username@remote-server:/path/to/directory ~/Downloads
```

You can also copy multiple files and directories by listing them, for example:

```
scp username@remote-server:/path/to/file1.txt /path/to/file2.txt /path/to/directory1/ ~/Downloads
```

You also can specify a different port number if the remote server uses a non-default port by using -P option:

```
scp -P 22 username@remote-server:/path/to/file.txt ~/Downloads
```

Please note that these commands require a remote server with the appropriate permissions and access to be set up, and also make sure you have the correct login credentials to access the remote server. Also, the **scp** command encrypts the data as it is transferred, providing an additional layer of security.

Archiving Folders

Sometimes we want to back up a folder by creating an archive. We might want to email it or upload it to a public server, or just simply copy it to a flash drive. If the goal is to keep the files together, an archive is perfect. If only I could remember what that command syntax is.

I asked for both the commands to archive and unarchive a given directory.

Archive the src directory using tar and gzip

To archive the **src** directory using **tar** and **gzip**, you can use the following command:

```
tar -czvf src.tar.gz src/
```

This command creates a new archive file called **src.tar.gz** that contains the contents of the **src** directory. The **-c** option tells **tar** to create a new archive, the **-z** option tells it to use **gzip** to compress the archive, and the **-v** option tells it to display verbose information about the progress of the archive creation. The **-f** option specifies the name and location of the archive file.

You can also use **tar** with **gzip** with the following command

tar -zcvf src.tar.gz src/

It will produce the same result.

Please note that this command will create the archive file in the current directory, you can specify a different directory to save the archive file. Also, the original **src** directory will not be deleted, if you want to delete it after archiving you can add --**remove-files** option

tar -czvf src.tar.gz --remove-files src/

This command will archive the src directory and remove the original directory after archiving it.

This is the first time I have seen ChatGPT provide the exact same information as an alternative to its first suggestion. Notice that the first two commands are identical except for the ordering of parameters, which is irrelevant. It's literally the same command.

I do appreciate the third option it gave, though. I was not aware of the --remove-files option.

I then asked it to uncompress the tar file. I admit that I was not prepared for the tutorial it generated.

To uncompress a **.tar.gz** file, you can use the following command:

tar -xzvf src.tar.gz

This command tells **tar** to extract the contents of the **src.tar.gz** file, the **-x** option tells it to extract the archive, the **-z** option tells it to use **gzip** to decompress the archive, and the **-v** option tells it to display verbose information about the progress of the extraction. The **-f** option specifies the name and location of the archive file.

You can also use the following command

tar -xvf src.tar.gz
This command will also extract the contents of the **src.tar.gz** file, but you need to specify that the file is gzipped by adding the **-z** option
tar -xvzf src.tar.gz
This command will extract the contents of the archive to the current directory, if you want to extract the files to a different directory you can use the **-C** option
tar -xvzf src.tar.gz -C /path/to/directory
This command will extract the files to the directory **/path/to/directory**. Please note that the extracted files will have the same permissions and ownership as the original files, if you want to change the permissions or ownership of the extracted files you can use the **--no-same-permissions** and **--no-same-owner** options.
tar -xvzf src.tar.gz --no-same-permissions --no-same-owner
This command will extract the files with the current user's permissions and ownership. Also, after extracting the files you can delete the original archive file by adding **-k** option
tar -xvzf src.tar.gz -k
This command will extract the files and keep the original archive file. It's important to note that tar.gz files are also known as tarballs, they are a combination of tar archive and gzip compression, the **.tar** file contains the files and the **.gz** file is the compression. It's important to use both options -x and -z to extract and decompress the file respectively.

Once again, it managed to get confused and

essentially gave me the same command for two different options. Otherwise, I think it did a thorough job explaining things.

GitHub SSH Key

I don't know about you, but I always have to look up how to create a new SSH key for GitHub using `git+ssh` protocol.

ChatGPT suggested that I use my email address as a comment and gave me a complete example. It also split the process into two commands instead a one, as I would have expected.

Create and copy a new ssh key for github to the clipboard

To create and copy a new SSH key for use with GitHub on macOS, you can use the **ssh-keygen** and **pbcopy** command. Here is an example of how to create a new SSH key and copy it to the clipboard:

Open the Terminal and generate a new SSH key:

```
ssh-keygen -t rsa -b 4096 -C "your_email@example.com"
```

This command creates a new RSA key with a 4096-bit key size, and associates the email "your_email@example.com" with the key as a comment.

When prompted, you can press Enter to accept the default location and file name for the key, or enter a new location and file name.

After the key is generated, you can copy the key to your clipboard using the **pbcopy** command:

```
pbcopy < ~/.ssh/id_rsa.pub
```

This command copies the contents of the file "~/.ssh/id_rsa.pub" to the clipboard.

> Go to your GitHub settings, under SSH and GPG keys, click on "New SSH Key" button.
>
> Give a title to the key, and paste the key on the "Key" field, press "Add SSH key" button.
>
> You can test the connection by running **ssh -T git@github.com**
>
> Please note that **pbcopy** command only works on macOS and is used to copy data to the clipboard. On other operating systems, the command may differ and you may need to use **xclip** or **xsel** to copy the key to the clipboard.

I love that ChatGPT goes above and beyond the actual command, providing examples, options, and even caveats.

Commands Specific to macOS

So far, I've been impressed with what ChatGPT has been able to do. There are other commands that I have a hard time remembering, particularly commands on macOS that manipulate media files. Let's see how it did with some of those.

Convert JPEG to PNG

Here is the first, asking it to convert a folder of JPEG files to PNG format.

> Convert all jpg files in the current directory to png files
>
> You can use the command-line tool **convert** from ImageMagick to convert all JPG files in the current directory to PNG files. Here is an example of how to use **convert** to convert all JPG files to PNG files:
>
> ```
> for file in *.jpg; do convert "$file" "${file%.jpg}.png"; done
> ```
>
> This command will loop through all files in the current

directory that have a **.jpg** extension, run the **convert** command on each file, and save the output to a new file with the same name but with a **.png** extension.

Alternatively, you can use **find** and **mogrify** command from ImageMagick:

find . -name "*.jpg" -exec mogrify -format png {} +

This command will search for all **.jpg** files in the current directory and its subdirectories and change their format to **.png** and overwrite the original files.

Please note that this will overwrite the original JPG files. If you want to keep the original files, you can modify the command to save the output to a different location or with a different file name.

ChatGPT told me that the convert command comes from ImageMagick, which I didn't have (and possibly have never heard of). Deciding not to give up just yet, I asked it how to install ImageMagick.

How do I install ImageMagick?

To install ImageMagick on macOS, you can use the package manager Homebrew. Here are the steps to install ImageMagick using Homebrew:

Install Homebrew if you haven't already by running the following command in the terminal:

/bin/bash -c "$(curl -fsSL https://raw.githubusercontent.com/Homebrew/install/HEAD/install.sh)"

Once Homebrew is installed, you can use it to install ImageMagick by running the following command in the terminal:

brew install imagemagick

After the installation is complete, you can check that it was successful by running the following command:

```
convert -version
```

This will display the version of ImageMagick that you have installed.

Another way to install ImageMagick on macOS is to download the binary package from the official website and install it manually. You can find the binary package here: https://imagemagick.org/script/download.php#macosx

Please note that you may need to add the ImageMagick binaries to your system's PATH for the **convert** and **mogrify** command to be recognized by the terminal.

Extract Audio from Video Files

As expected, ChatGPT gave me a lot of context, after suggesting the command, and also explaining what I needed to understand about it.

Extract audio from all the mp4 files in the folder

You can use the command-line tool **ffmpeg** to extract the audio from all MP4 files in a folder on macOS. Here is an example of how to use **ffmpeg** to extract the audio from all MP4 files in the current directory and save it as an MP3 file:

```
for file in *.mp4; do ffmpeg -i "$file" -vn -acodec libmp3lame -ac 2 -q:a 4 -y "${file%.mp4}.mp3"; done
```

This command will loop through all files in the current directory that have a **.mp4** extension, run the **ffmpeg** command on each file, and save the audio output to a new file with the same name but with a **.mp3** extension.

This command uses the -i option to specify the input file, the -vn option to disable the video stream, the -acodec option to specify the audio codec, -ac 2 to specify the number of audio channels, -q:a 4 to specify the audio quality and -y to overwriting output files.

You can change the output file format and codec by changing the **mp3** and **libmp3lame** accordingly.

Please note that you may need to install **ffmpeg** in your system if it is not already installed. You can install **ffmpeg** using Homebrew by running the following command in the terminal:

brew install ffmpeg

Also, please note that this command will overwrite any existing files with the same name. If you want to keep the original files, you can modify the command to save the output to a different location or with a different file name.

The command ChatGPT gave is complete, but its explanation is misleading. Or maybe I simply read it wrong. The -y parameter will automatically overwrite any existing files on output, but the command is not destructive to the input files.

My final test was to try to extract audio using avconvert, another command on macOS. Apparently, this command no longer exists, which ChatGPT was happy to explain to me when I asked about it.

What is avconvert?

avconv is a command-line tool similar to **ffmpeg** that can be used to convert multimedia files. To extract the audio from a video file using **avconv** on macOS, you can use the following command:

avconv -i inputfile.mp4 -vn -acodec libmp3lame -ac 2 -q:a 4 -y outputfile.mp3

This command uses the **-i** option to specify the input file, the

-vn option to disable the video stream, the -acodec option to specify the audio codec as libmp3lame, the -ac 2 option to specify the number of audio channels, the -q:a 4 option to specify the audio quality and the -y option to overwrite output files if they already exist.

You can change the input and output file name and format accordingly, also you can change the codec and quality options as you need.

Please note that you may need to install avconv in your system if it is not already installed. You can install avconv using Homebrew by running the following command in the terminal:

> brew install libav

Please note that avconv and ffmpeg are similar but not exactly the same, and their syntax and options may differ slightly. Some options or codecs that work with ffmpeg may not work with avconv, and vice versa. Also, ffmpeg is more commonly used and has more active development than avconv, but both of them can be used to extract audio from a video file.

Note that it didn't answer the question that I asked, or so I thought. Confused and mildly curious, I then asked for clarification.

> What is the difference between avconv and avconvert?

avconv and avconvert are actually the same thing, avconv is the command-line tool for the libav library, that is a fork of the ffmpeg library. avconv was the command-line tool for the libav library and it's the equivalent of the ffmpeg command-line tool for the ffmpeg library, but the libav project was discontinued in 2018 and now the libav developers recommend using ffmpeg instead of avconv. avconvert is a typo or a misspelling of avconv, and both commands can be used to perform the same tasks. The avconv tool has been

> replaced by **ffmpeg**, but you might find some old resources or scripts that use **avconv** or **avconvert**.
>
> In summary, **avconv** and **avconvert** are the same command-line tool, but the **libav** project was discontinued in 2018 and now it's recommended to use **ffmpeg** instead of **avconv**.

What amazed me is that I thought avconvert was the current and correct command to use. Apparently, I was mistaken on both counts.

Parting Thoughts

While using AI tools can potentially save time and effort, it is important to assess the quality of the generated commands and ensure they are safe and effective. The output from ChatGPT complete and provides appropriate context, but I expected that.

ChatGPT is an advanced AI model that is capable of understanding and responding to complex and nuanced questions. It can provide accurate and reliable answers to your questions, and its output is more detailed and comprehensive.

In addition to the difference in output quality, another aspect to consider is the area of expertise of each tool. ChatGPT is a general-purpose language model that has been trained on a vast amount of text data, making it a good choice when the subject matter may be unfamiliar, or when you need an explanation or clarification. It is good at providing a comprehensive understanding of a topic, and it can be used for a wide range of tasks, including language translation, text generation, and question answering.

As you will continue to see, it can help you with

your coding tasks by suggesting snippets of code, providing documentation, and even completing your code for you.

COMMON ALGORITHMS

Image by Markus Spiske from Pixabay

One of my favorite uses for AI is to have it generate code for common algorithms. In this chapter, I will highlight some real-world situations where I have used it to solve common problems.

IIFE

Do you know what an IIFE is in JavaScript? Well, just ask ChatGPT!

> What's an IIFE in Javascript, why would I need one, and how would I create one?

IIFE stands for Immediately Invoked Function Expression. It is a common design pattern used in JavaScript to create a private scope for your code and avoid polluting the global namespace with variables and functions.

You might use an IIFE in situations where you need to encapsulate some code and prevent it from affecting other code on the page. For example, you might use an IIFE to define a module in your application, where the module's code is contained within the IIFE's private scope.

To create an IIFE, you simply define a function expression and wrap it in parentheses to make it an expression. You can then immediately invoke the function by appending a pair of parentheses after it, like this:

```
(function() {
  // your code here
})();
```

In this example, an anonymous function is defined and immediately invoked. The function creates a private scope for the code inside it, preventing any variables or functions declared within it from leaking into the global scope.

Note that the parentheses around the function expression are necessary, because they cause the function to be interpreted as an expression rather than a declaration. Without these parentheses, the JavaScript parser would interpret the function as a function declaration, which can only be used in certain contexts.

That's a pretty impressive explanation. It actually gave me a longer explanation, but I pared it down for you.

Granted, with TypeScript, we hardly need to use IIFEs anymore. In fact, what if we asked ChatGPT to convert its last IIFE into an equivalent TypeScript class?

> What would be the equivalent of that code if we were to use classes in TypeScript instead?
>
> If you were to use classes in TypeScript to achieve a similar result as the IIFE example, you could define a class and use the **constructor** method to execute your code.
>
> Here's an example:

```
class MyClass {
  constructor() {
    // your code here
  }
}
new MyClass();
```

> In this example, the **MyClass** constructor function is executed immediately when an instance of the class is created using the **new** keyword.
>
> You could also pass arguments to the constructor method, like this:

```
class MyClass {
  constructor(arg1, arg2) {
    // your code here
  }
}
new MyClass(val1, val2);
```

> In this case, the arguments **val1** and **val2** are passed to the constructor method as **arg1** and **arg2**, respectively.

> Using classes in TypeScript provides additional benefits, such as better type checking and encapsulation, as well as the ability to define public and private members. However, the overall goal of both the IIFE and class examples is the same: to encapsulate your code and prevent it from affecting other code on the page.

Notice I didn't have to restate my request, but simply asked it to rewrite "that code." This is our first example of ChatGPT remembering the context of the conversation.

Array Functions

ChatGPT is really good at helping manipulate arrays. All you need to do is ask.

Reduce

For some reason, I can never remember how to use JavaScript's `reduce` function to calculate the sum of the items in an array. Consider the following array of "puzzles." This is a I snippet from my game Foreword, a game of word squares.

```
// Partial array of "puzzles" for this example
private demoPuzzles: Puzzle[] = [
  { id:88, size: 4, solution: ['abetbabeebontent'] },
  { id:89, size: 4, solution: ['icedcaveevendent'] },
  { id:90, size: 8, solution: ['abetracemirestun', 'armsbaitecruteen'] },
  { id:91, size: 8, solution: ['cageheaturicmyth', 'chumaerygaitetch'] }
];
```

Notice that some puzzles have one solution, and some have two. My actual array of puzzles has thousands of elements.

Now let's assume I want to count the total number of solutions in my puzzle array. I provided ChatGPT with a simple prompt.

> Count the total number of solutions in the demo Puzzle array
>
> In JavaScript, you can use the reduce method on the array to count the total number of solutions in the demoPuzzles array. reduce works by applying a function against an accumulator and each element in the array (from left to right) to reduce it to a single output value. In this case, the accumulator is a count of the total number of solutions, and for each puzzle in the array, the number of solutions in that puzzle is added to the count.
>
> ```
> let totalSolutions = this.demoPuzzles.reduce((count, puzzle) => {
>   return count + puzzle.solution.length;
> }, 0);
> console.log(totalSolutions);
> ```
>
> This code defines an initial count of 0 and then, for each puzzle, adds the number of solutions in that puzzle to the count. The result is the total number of solutions in the array.
>
> Note: Since you are using a private member of a class, this code should be inside a method of the class. If demoPuzzles is not a member of a class, you can remove the this. before demoPuzzles.

Yeah, I could have used a `for` loop, or looked up the syntax of `Array.reduce`, but ChatGPT did this for me, with nothing more than a prompt. To me, that's productive!

Notice that last warning. I hadn't even realized I had

marked it as private, but ChatGPT recognized it and told me how to deal with it.

Filter

Next, imagine I want to find all the puzzles in the array of size 4. When I gave the prompt to ChatGPT, it went in a slightly different direction than I was expecting.

> Given an array that looks like the following array, find all puzzles of size 4 or 8. (I then pasted the puzzles array).
>
> To find all puzzles of size 4 or 8, you can use the **filter** method on the **demoPuzzles** array and provide a callback function that checks the size of each puzzle:
>
> ```
> const filteredPuzzles = demoPuzzles.filter(puzzle => puzzle.size === 4 || puzzle.size === 8);
> ```
>
> This will return a new array that contains only the puzzles that have a size of 4 or 8.
>
> You could also use the forEach method and check the size of each puzzle, then push the matching puzzles into a new array:
>
> ```
> const filteredPuzzles = [];
> demoPuzzles.forEach(puzzle => {
>   if (puzzle.size === 4 || puzzle.size === 8) {
>     filteredPuzzles.push(puzzle);
>   }
> });
> ```
>
> This achieves the same result as the **filter** method.
>
> In either case, the resulting **filteredPuzzles** array will contain only the puzzles of size 4 or 8.

In this case, ChatGPT took me literally, giving me a

way to find puzzles of either size 4 or of size 8. The odd thing is that the code it gave me will produce an array with the identical contents as the original, which is not at all helpful.

Sort

What if I wanted to sort the array? I know that JavaScript has a `sort` function and that it takes a callback function that describes how the sort should be done. But maybe I can't quite remember the syntax. ChatGPT offered me this response.

> // Sort the puzzles by size, with the largest first
>
> ```
> const sortedPuzzles = demoPuzzles.sort((a, b) => b.size - a.size);
> ```
>
> This will return a new array that contains the puzzles sorted by size, with the largest first.
>
> In this example, the **sort** method takes a callback function that compares the **size** property of the **a** and **b** objects. By subtracting **a.size** from **b.size**, we ensure that the puzzles are sorted in descending order based on size.

I still love that ChatGPT offers an explanation for its suggestions. This makes it the perfect learning companion.

Array as a Stack or a Queue

Sometimes we want to implement a stack or a queue with arrays. ChatGPT can help with that also. In fact, it gave me a complete set of strongly typed TypeScript functions when I asked it to do so:

> Generate a set of strongly typed TypeScript functions to treat the array like a stack or queue.
>
> ```
> type Puzzle = { id: number; size: number; solution: string[] };
> ```

```
function pushToStack(stack: Puzzle[], puzzle: Puzzle): Puzzle[] {
  return [...stack, puzzle];
}
function popFromStack(stack: Puzzle[]): [Puzzle | undefined, Puzzle[]] {
  const poppedPuzzle = stack[stack.length - 1];
  const newStack = stack.slice(0, stack.length - 1);
  return [poppedPuzzle, newStack];
}
function enqueue(queue: Puzzle[], puzzle: Puzzle): Puzzle[] {
  return [...queue, puzzle];
}
function dequeue(queue: Puzzle[]): [Puzzle | undefined, Puzzle[]] {
  const dequeuedPuzzle = queue[0];
  const newQueue = queue.slice(1);
  return [dequeuedPuzzle, newQueue];
}
```

As usual, it provided a complete explanation for each function, though I did not reproduce it here.

Array to Hash

In one of my projects, I queried a remote web service to retrieve customer and sales information, which was returned in data structure that looked something like the following.

```
"orders": [
```

```
{
  "id": "order1",
  "customerName": "John Smith",
  "productName": "Shirt",
  "quantity": 2,
  "price": 25
},
{
  "id": "order2",
  "customerName": "Jane Doe",
  "productName": "Pants",
  "quantity": 1,
  "price": 40
},
{
  "id": "order3",
  "customerName": "Bob Johnson",
  "productName": "Socks",
  "quantity": 3,
  "price": 10
}
]
```

Notice that `orders` is an array, with each order being a self-contained object in the array. Now imagine that there are hundreds or thousands of such orders. If I wanted to grab just `order72`, I would have to traverse the entire array. If the data structure were a hash instead, with each order having its *id* as the key, it would be much simpler (and faster) to get any arbitrary element.

I could very quickly come up with code that loops through the entire array and generates a new hash object, but this is the sort of mundane task at which ChatGPT excels. This is the prompt I gave it, followed by the code it produced.

ChatGPT offered to use the `reduce` function, which honestly never occurred to me. As I told you before, it's not a function that I'm good at. It's one of my (many?) blind spots.

> I have an array in TypeScript with the following shape. (I pasted the above JSON here). I want to convert it from an array to a hash array so that can address each object by its "id".
>
> You can convert the array to a hash array by using the **reduce** method and creating a new object with the "id" property as the key. Here's an example:
>
> ```
> const hashArray = orders.reduce((acc, config) => {
>   acc[config.id] = config;
>   return acc;
> }, {});
> ```
>
> Now you can access each object by its "id" like this: **hashArray["order2"]**.

I then further refined it by asking for a standalone function, which it created for me (not shown).

String Manipulation

Do you find yourself manipulating text often? I know I do. Extracting smaller bits of text from long inputs, determining whether one string exists inside another, dealing with padding, etc. Those sorts of things are reasonably straightforward, but I prefer not to type this stuff if I don't have to.

String searches

Consider the problem of finding every occurrence of a word inside a longer string. How would ChatGPT approach it?

> const text = "The quick brown fox jumps over the lazy dog.";
>
> Find all occurrences of the substring "the" (case-insensitive)
>
> In JavaScript, you can find all occurrences of a substring in a string using the match() method, in combination with a regular expression. The i flag in the regular expression is used for case-insensitive searching.
>
> Here's an example of how you can find all occurrences of the substring "the" in the provided string:
>
> ```
> const text = "The quick brown fox jumps over the lazy dog.";
> const substring = "the";
> const regex = new RegExp(substring, "gi");
> const matches = text.match(regex);
> console.log(matches);
> ```
>
> This will print an array with all occurrences of "the" in the text, regardless of case. The g in the regular expression ensures that all matches are found, rather than stopping after the first match.
>
> If you just want the count of occurrences, you can check the length of the returned array, like so:

```
const count = matches ? matches.length : 0;
console.log(count);
```

This code checks whether matches is not null before trying to access its length property because match() returns null when there are no matches. If matches is null, the count is set to 0.

ChatGPT went directly to regular expressions. I'll dive deeper into regexes later in the book.

GitHub Copilot

I want to take a detour here and show what GitHub Copilot did here, as it highlights an amazing use of ChatGPT. When I asked Copilot for the same type of code, it also used a regular expression, but it went in an entirely different direction.

```
const regex = /the/gi;
let m;
while ((m = regex.exec(text)) !== null) {
  // This is necessary to avoid infinite loops with zero-width matches
  if (m.index === regex.lastIndex) {
    regex.lastIndex++;
  }
  // The result can be accessed through the `m`-variable.
  m.forEach((match, groupIndex) => {
    console.log(`Found match, group ${groupIndex}: ${match}`);
  });
}
```

In all honesty, I'm not entirely sure I understand what Copilot gave me there. For fun, I pasted its code sample into ChatGPT and asked it to explain it to me. This is what it said.

> This JavaScript code finds all occurrences of the substring "the" in a given piece of text using regular expressions, and logs the matches to the console. Here's a breakdown of how it works:
>
> const regex = /the/gi; - This line creates a regular expression regex that matches the substring "the" with the /the/ syntax. The g and i flags are used to perform a global search and a case-insensitive search, respectively.
>
> let m; - This line declares a variable m without initializing it.
>
> while ((m = regex.exec(text)) !== null) { - This line sets m to the result of calling the regex.exec(text) method, which returns an array of information about the next match of the regular expression in the text string. The while loop continues as long as m is not null.
>
> if (m.index === regex.lastIndex) { regex.lastIndex++; } - This line checks whether the match is a zero-width match (i.e., an empty string), and if so, increments the lastIndex property of the regex object to avoid an infinite loop.
>
> m.forEach((match, groupIndex) => { console.log(Found match, group ${groupIndex}: ${match}); }); - This line loops through each match in the m array using the forEach() method, and logs each match and its group index to the console using a template literal.
>
> Overall, this code is a more advanced version of the previous code examples, using the regex.exec() method to iterate over each match and access its properties. The use of forEach() allows for more fine-grained control over the output and provides access to the match's group index, which can be useful when working with more complex regular expressions.

Do you see what it did? Read that final paragraph carefully. ChatGPT recognized that the code I pasted from Copilot was related to my original question, and then explained that it was a more advanced example of the same concept. Truly amazing!

Removing whitespace

Sometimes, you may be faced with a lengthy piece of text with too much whitespace. Given such a string, how would you remove its excess whitespace, while preserving the important text?

For this example, I asked ChatGPT to generate some sample "lorem ipsum" text with lots of extra whitespace.

```
const loremIpsumWithWhitespace = `
Lorem ipsum     dolor sit amet, consectetur adipiscing elit. Fusce molestie turpis    nec    felis malesuada accumsan. Vestibulum  tincidunt lacus nec nulla dignissim blandit. Morbi tristique, enim eu imperdiet luctus, nisl turpis aliquam nunc, eu interdum purus velit   quis velit.    Curabitur vel semper tellus,  at iaculis lectus.  Morbi sed lectus   ac nibh eleifend tristique.  Praesent sagittis elit vel dui consequat,  eu maximus purus molestie. Integer varius  pharetra odio, non vestibulum urna lobortis et.  Sed et eleifend lorem, quis mollis ipsum.

Pellentesque     consectetur   mauris sed risus laoreet,   vel malesuada augue convallis.    Nullam vestibulum commodo metus, id tristique est suscipit id. Etiam pretium sagittis malesuada.   Vivamus sit amet mi lorem.    Etiam hendrerit euismod libero, nec   accumsan massa laoreet vel.    Donec viverra felis et urna fringilla, non convallis tellus egestas. Suspendisse faucibus quam in erat sagittis   dignissim. Duis maximus risus sit amet eros bibendum feugiat.`;
```

Next, I asked for a generic function that would accept that type of input and return the string with all the insignificant whitespace removed.

```
function removeInsignificantWhitespace(text) {
  // Replace all whitespace characters with a single space
  const stripped = text.replace(/\s+/g, " ");
  // Remove leading/trailing spaces and line breaks
  return stripped.trim();
}
```

This function works by first using a regular expression (/\s+/g) to match all occurrences of one or more whitespace characters (spaces, tabs, line breaks, etc.) and replacing them with a single space character using the **replace()** method.

The resulting string is then passed to the **trim()** method, which removes any leading or trailing spaces or line breaks.

This ensures that the final output contains only the necessary whitespace characters (e.g., spaces between words) and no unnecessary ones.

Whitespace Padding

Now, let's consider the puzzle array. If I wanted to generate some pretty formatting using only text in a fixed-width font, how might I do that? ChatGPT gave me the following function, along with a sample of what the output would look like:

Generate some pretty formatting using only text in a fixed-width font

```
const printTable = (puzzles: Puzzle[]): void => {
  console.log('ID Size Solution');
```

```
  console.log('--------------------');
  puzzles.forEach(puzzle => {
      console.log(`${puzzle.id.toString().padEnd(4, ' ')}${puzzle.size.toString().padEnd(6, ' ')}${puzzle.solution[0]}`);
  });
};
printTable(demoPuzzles);
```

This code will output the **demoPuzzles** array as a table with fixed-width font, like this:

```
ID  Size Solution
--------------------
88  4    abetbabeebontent
89  4    icedcaveevendent
90  8    abetracemirestun
91  8    cageheaturicmyth
```

Generating CSV Files

What if I wanted to output the array as a comma-separated file instead?

ChatGPT gave me some pretty good code, and it even accounted for potential commas in my puzzle fields.

```
import * as fs from 'fs';
const generateCSV = (puzzles: Puzzle[]): void => {
  const header = 'id,size,solution\n';
    const rows = puzzles.map(puzzle => `${puzzle.id},${puzzle.size},"${puzzle.solution.join(';')}"\n`);
  const csv = header + rows.join('');
```

```
fs.writeFileSync('puzzles.csv', csv);
};
generateCSV(demoPuzzles);
```

Notice that its solution assumed I'm using Node, in that it uses the `fs` library. Fortunately, ChatGPT took extra care to inform me that I would need the `fs` module from NodeJS.

> Note that in order to run this code, you will need to have the **fs** module and the Node.js runtime installed.

Generate HTML

I could also ask it to generate HTML for me. ChatGPT did exactly what I asked it to, again remembering the shape of my puzzles array and objects.

> Create a function in JavaScript that will output the puzzles array as an HTML table

```
function printTable(puzzles) {
  const table = document.createElement('table');
  const headerRow = document.createElement('tr');
  const idHeader = document.createElement('th');
  const sizeHeader = document.createElement('th');
  const solutionHeader = document.createElement('th');
  idHeader.textContent = 'ID';
  sizeHeader.textContent = 'Size';
  solutionHeader.textContent = 'Solution';
  headerRow.appendChild(idHeader);
  headerRow.appendChild(sizeHeader);
```

```javascript
  headerRow.appendChild(solutionHeader);
  table.appendChild(headerRow);
  puzzles.forEach(puzzle => {
    const row = document.createElement('tr');
    const idCell = document.createElement('td');
    const sizeCell = document.createElement('td');
    const solutionCell = document.createElement('td');
    idCell.textContent = puzzle.id;
    sizeCell.textContent = puzzle.size;
    solutionCell.textContent = puzzle.solution.join(';');
    row.appendChild(idCell);
    row.appendChild(sizeCell);
    row.appendChild(solutionCell);
    table.appendChild(row);
  });
  document.body.appendChild(table);
}
printTable(demoPuzzles);
```

Here I think it may have outdone itself. I was expecting to see a bunch of hard-coded strings with HTML characters. I didn't expect it to use DOM manipulation, but of course, that might be the better solution in many cases.

Conclusion

This chapter focused primarily on array and string manipulation, which is what most of my day-to-day work entails. You may have different algorithms you work with regularly. Rest assured that either of these tools will save you a lot of typing. The important thing to keep in mind is that the prompt is just as important as the language you ask them to use.

Sometimes you have to try multiple prompts to get the right code. Finally, make sure you validate the correctness of the code. Either tool can create code that looks great but doesn't account for edge cases.

Remember that at the end of the day, you're the programmer, not the AI.

LEARNING RXJS

Image by Gerd Altmann from Pixabay

Working with ChatGPT on common algorithms got me thinking that it could be very useful tools for learning Reactive Extensions for JavaScript (RxJS), or at least to help me remember some of its non-obvious syntax.

A lot of people don't like to use RxJS, thinking it's too complicated. They tend to avoid it, which I believe is a shame. Yes, RxJS can have a steep learning curve, but learning to think "reactively" and using RxJS effectively have been worth the effort. I wondered how useful ChatGPT could be in helping others to learn RxJS.

For this chapter, I'm going to continue using that array of puzzles from before. In case you need a refresher, it looks like this:

```
Partial array of "puzzles" for this example
private demoPuzzles: Puzzle[] = [
  { id:88, size: 4, solution: ['abetbabeebontent'] },
  { id:89, size: 4, solution: ['icedcaveevendent'] },
  { id:90, size: 8, solution: ['abetracemirestun', 'armsbaitecruteen'] },
  { id:91, size: 8, solution: ['cageheaturicmyth', 'chumaerygaitetch'] }
];
```

from and of

Sticking with the above array of puzzles, let's imagine that the puzzles are part of a game, and that they exist as a stream of Observables. Further, assume that the game gets them from some outside source. Don't worry about where they are coming from; that isn't the point here. Every time a new puzzle is presented, the game will do "something" with it.

So, I asked ChatGPT to do just that. This is my prompt and the code it wrote for me:

```
Create a new observable from the demo Puzzle array

In TypeScript or JavaScript, you would use the RxJS (Reactive Extensions for JavaScript) library to create Observables. Observables are used for handling asynchronous data streams.

First, make sure you have the RxJS library installed in your project. If not, you can add it using npm:
```

```
npm install rxjs
```

Then, you can create an Observable from the demo Puzzle array as follows:

```
import { Observable, from } from 'rxjs';

// Assuming this is your puzzle array
private demoPuzzles: Puzzle[] = [
  { id:88, size: 4, solution: ['abetbabeebontent'] },
  { id:89, size: 4, solution: ['icedcaveevendent'] },
  { id:90, size: 8, solution: ['abetracemirestun', 'armsbaitecruteen'] },
  { id:91, size: 8, solution: ['cageheaturicmyth', 'chumaerygaitetch'] }
  // ...
];

// Create an Observable
let puzzleObservable: Observable<Puzzle> = from(this.demoPuzzles);

// Subscribe to the Observable
puzzleObservable.subscribe(puzzle => console.log(puzzle));
```

In this code, the from function from RxJS is used to convert the array into an Observable. The subscribe method is then used to subscribe to the Observable, which will output each puzzle to the console as it is emitted.

Remember, Observables are lazy, meaning they don't do anything until you subscribe to them. Once you subscribe, the Observable will emit each item in the array one at a time.

The type Puzzle in Observable<Puzzle> is assuming that you have a Puzzle interface or class defined in your TypeScript

> code. If not, you might need to replace Puzzle with the correct type, or use any if the type is not important.
>
> Note: If the demoPuzzles is not in a class, you can omit this..

Perfect! The RxJS `from` function creates a new Observable from an array, emitting a new value for each element of the array. That is exactly what I wanted.

There is another RxJS operator, `of`, that can also create an Observable from an array. Though it would have been valid to use that, `of` creates a single Observable from that emits once, containing the entire array. That is not what I wanted, and somehow ChatGPT knew (or guessed) that.

I also appreciate that it wants to make sure that I know how to install RxJS into my project. That's a nice touch that I never got from Copilot or GPT 3.5.

filter

Now that we have an Observable let's do something with it. Let's start with a couple of the simpler and more common RxJS operators: `map` and `filter`.

The RxJS `filter` operator is used to do what its name implies: filter an existing stream to include only those items that match some provided criteria.

What if the game player only wants to see puzzles of size 4? Can we get it to do that for us? Here is the prompt I typed and the code ChatGPT generated in reply:

> Filter puzzles to only those of size 4

In JavaScript, you can use the filter() method to create a new array that includes only the elements of the original array that satisfy a certain condition. In your case, you want to include only the puzzles that have a size of 4. Here's how you can do it:

```
let sizeFourPuzzles = this.demoPuzzles.filter(puzzle => puzzle.size === 4);
console.log(sizeFourPuzzles);
```

This code goes through each puzzle in demoPuzzles and checks if its size is equal to 4. If it is, the puzzle is included in the new sizeFourPuzzles array. If it's not, the puzzle is not included.

As before, if demoPuzzles is not a member of a class, you can remove the this. before demoPuzzles.

If you are working with Observables, and you have an Observable of Puzzles, you can use the filter operator from RxJS to filter out the Puzzles:

```
import { filter } from 'rxjs/operators';
let sizeFourPuzzles$ = puzzleObservable.pipe(
  filter(puzzle => puzzle.size === 4)
);
sizeFourPuzzles$.subscribe(puzzle => console.log(puzzle));
```

In this case, sizeFourPuzzles$ is a new Observable that will emit only the puzzles with a size of 4. The $ at the end of sizeFourPuzzles$ is a naming convention used in the RxJS community to indicate that a variable is an Observable.

What did it give us? It created a new Observable called `sizeFourPuzzles$`, this time adding a common naming convention of appending a dollar sign to the names of variables representing Observables. I was somewhat surprised it didn't do that at first.

It also correctly understands that to use the *filter* operator, we first have to use the RxJS *pipe* function. Any time you are working with an RxJS Observable, and you want to act on it before subscribing to the value stream, you need to pass a list of operators into the *pipe* function.

Next, to select the puzzles of size 4, it correctly deduced that I would need the *filter* operator, which takes a callback function defining how each item in the stream should be matched. If it looks familiar, it's because it works exactly like *Array.filter*.

You might be thinking that I cheated a bit by using the word "Filter" in my comment. What would happen if I used a different phrase? Well, I decided to find out.

map

Let's see what happens if we want only a part of each of the above puzzles. Maybe we are only going to display the first solution of the puzzle as it is emitted.

Any time you want to coerce one object into another, you would first reach for the *map* operator, which works very similarly to the JavaScript Array function of the same name.

As with the prior examples, here are my prompt and the generated code:

> Display only the first solution of each puzzle
>
> In JavaScript, you can use the map() method to create a new array with the results of calling a function for every array element. In this case, you can use it to create a new array that includes only the first solution of each puzzle. Here's how you

can do it:

```
let firstSolutions = this.demoPuzzles.map(puzzle => puzzle.solution[0]);
console.log(firstSolutions);
```

This code goes through each puzzle in demoPuzzles and gets the first solution of each puzzle (at index 0). These first solutions are then included in the new firstSolutions array.

As before, if demoPuzzles is not a member of a class, you can remove the this. before demoPuzzles.

If you are working with Observables, and you have an Observable of Puzzles, you can use the map operator from RxJS to transform the Puzzles:

```
import { map } from 'rxjs/operators';

let firstSolutions$ = puzzleObservable.pipe(
  map(puzzle => puzzle.solution[0])
);

firstSolutions$.subscribe(solution => console.log(solution));
```

In this case, firstSolutions$ is a new Observable that will emit only the first solution of each puzzle. The $ at the end of firstSolutions$ is a naming convention used in the RxJS community to indicate that a variable is an Observable.

Do you see what it did there? It wasn't entirely sure whether I meant to use the original puzzle array or the observable it had just created for me. What did it do? It gave me the code for both! As I have previously pointed out, this shows that ChatGPT is aware of the context of your prior conversations.

I think the only disagreement I have is the name `firstSolution$`, but right now I can't think of a better one.

At this point, I have an Observable that is filtered and mapped to only give me the first solution of size-4 puzzles as they are emitted.

Could it combine them for me?

What if I structured my prompt to try to get it to write the entire pipeline for me? Let's see how that would look.

> Give me the first solution of each size-4 puzzles
>
> In JavaScript, you can combine the filter() and map() methods to first filter the puzzles to include only those of size 4 and then map the result to include only the first solution of each puzzle. Here's how you can do it:
>
> ```
> let firstSolutionsOfFour = this.demoPuzzles
>   .filter(puzzle => puzzle.size === 4)
>   .map(puzzle => puzzle.solution[0]);
> console.log(firstSolutionsOfFour);
> ```
>
> This code first filters the puzzles to include only those of size 4, then maps the result to include only the first solution of each puzzle.
>
> As before, if demoPuzzles is not a member of a class, you can remove the this. before demoPuzzles.
>
> If you are working with Observables, you can use the filter and map operators from RxJS:
>
> ```
> import { filter, map } from 'rxjs/operators';
> let firstSolutionsOfFour$ = puzzleObservable.pipe(
>   filter(puzzle => puzzle.size === 4),
>   map(puzzle => puzzle.solution[0])
> ```

```
);
firstSolutionsOfFour$.subscribe(solution                                  =>
console.log(solution));
```

In this case, firstSolutionsOfFour$ is a new Observable that will emit only the first solution of each puzzle of size 4. The $ at the end of firstSolutionsOfFour$ is a naming convention used in the RxJS community to indicate that a variable is an Observable.

That's exactly what I wanted it to do. I really appreciate the way it doesn't simply assume what I want to do but gives me options. It also got my meaning on the first try, which is not what I experienced with other AI tools.

take

The `take` operator is used to select (or take) only a certain number of emissions from the observable and then automatically disconnect. ChatGPT knew exactly how to structure that for me.

This time, however, I decided to modify my prompt just a bit. We are working exclusively with Observables, so it might help the output if we tell it that.

For the rest of this discussion, until further notice, assuming I'm only working with the observables we created earlier. Take only the first two size 8 puzzles.

Given that we are now only working with Observables, you can take only the first two puzzles of size 8 using the filter and take operators from RxJS. Here's how you can do it:

```
import { filter, take } from 'rxjs/operators';
```

```
let firstTwoSizeEightPuzzles$ = puzzleObservable.pipe(
  filter(puzzle => puzzle.size === 8),
  take(2)
);
firstTwoSizeEightPuzzles$.subscribe(puzzle => console.log(puzzle));
```

In this code, firstTwoSizeEightPuzzles$ is a new Observable that is created from puzzleObservable by filtering to include only puzzles of size 8, then taking only the first two of these puzzles. The $ at the end of firstTwoSizeEightPuzzles$ is a naming convention used in the RxJS community to indicate that a variable is an Observable.

The subscribe() method is then used to subscribe to the Observable, which will output each of the first two puzzles of size 8 to the console as they are emitted.

Do you see how adding a little extra context can dramatically change how ChatGPT generated its answer? This is a small example of of "prompt engineering," and there has been a lot of research around it.

Don't be afraid to challenge it by giving it different context.

tap

Sometimes you want to see the values in an Observable stream without affecting the stream or any downstream operators. The **tap** operator is built for that exact scenario. Could I get it to rewrite my logging statement above to use tap?

> *Regenerate the last sample code, but log all puzzles to the console*

(not just the size-8 ones)

If you want to log all puzzles to the console, not just the size-8 ones, you can use the tap operator from RxJS. The tap operator allows you to perform side effects for each emission on the source Observable, but returns an Observable that is identical to the source.

Here's how you can modify the code to log all puzzles to the console:

```
import { filter, take, tap } from 'rxjs/operators';
let firstTwoSizeEightPuzzles$ = puzzleObservable.pipe(
  tap(puzzle => console.log('All puzzles:', puzzle)),
  filter(puzzle => puzzle.size === 8),
  take(2)
);
firstTwoSizeEightPuzzles$.subscribe(puzzle => console.log('Size-8 puzzles:', puzzle));
```

In this code, the tap operator is used to log all puzzles to the console before the filtering and taking operations are performed. The filter and take operators then work as before to create a new Observable that emits only the first two puzzles of size 8. The subscribe() method logs these puzzles to the console as they are emitted.

This way, all puzzles will be logged to the console, but only the first two puzzles of size 8 will be emitted by firstTwoSizeEightPuzzles$.

That looks exactly right, and what had expected (hoped?) it would generate.

What's the Takeaway?

Admittedly, there is a lot more to RxJS than the few

operators I used here. RxJS is huge, with more than 100 operators, though most developers use fewer than a dozen of them regularly. The goal of this chapter wasn't to perform an exhaustive test of RxJS.

Can it help someone learn RxJS or how to use it better? I think so, with a caveat. An RxJS novice just starting out may not have enough experience to know what to accept and when to try again.

My purpose was to see whether ChatGPT can help a novice developer get up to speed with RxJS, knowing only a little about what it can do. I will use more RxJS later, where the context is a little more appropriate.

ANGULAR'S HTTPCLIENT

Image by Gerd Altmann from Pixabay

Now let's consider Angular's HttpClient, which makes heavy use of RxJS. In fact, the HttpClient is often the first place the new Angular developer is introduced to RxJS. That can be a make or break experience.

So, I wanted to see how well it does with some of the common coding patterns we see when using Angular's HttpClient.

Even if you aren't an Angular developer, the process is worth understanding.

A Typical Angular Service

For this example, I decided to start with absolutely nothing and see exactly how little code I could write. I opened ChatGPT and started a brand new conversation, selecting GPT-4 as my model

Next, I entered the following prompt.

> Provide me an Angular service called ApiService
>
> Sure, here's a simple example of an Angular service named ApiService. In this example, we'll use the HttpClient module to make HTTP requests. This service is designed to interact with an API, with get and post methods as examples.
>
> ```
> import { Injectable } from '@angular/core';
> import { HttpClient } from '@angular/common/http';
> import { Observable } from 'rxjs';
> @Injectable({
>   providedIn: 'root'
> })
> export class ApiService {
>   private API_URL = 'http://localhost:3000/api/';
>   constructor(private http: HttpClient) { }
>   public get(endpoint: string): Observable<any> {
>     return this.http.get(this.API_URL + endpoint);
>   }
>   public post(endpoint: string, data: any): Observable<any> {
>     return this.http.post(this.API_URL + endpoint, data);
>   }
> }
> ```
>
> You can use this service in your components by injecting it in the constructor. Here is an example of how you might use this service in a component:

```
import { Component, OnInit } from '@angular/core';
import { ApiService } from './api.service';
@Component({
  selector: 'app-my-component',
  templateUrl: './my-component.component.html',
  styleUrls: ['./my-component.component.css']
})
export class MyComponent implements OnInit {
  constructor(private apiService: ApiService) { }
  ngOnInit() {
    this.apiService.get('endpoint').subscribe(data => {
      console.log(data);
    });
  }
}
```

Please replace 'http://localhost:3000/api/' and 'endpoint' with your actual API URL and endpoint. Also, it is a good practice to handle errors when making HTTP requests, you can use RxJS operators such as catchError for this purpose.

That's all pretty cool, but not really what I wanted. I can't complain too much, though, because I didn't give it anything else to go on. Let's see what else we can get it to do.

A Simple HTTP GET

Whenever I'm building a demo app, I always struggle with where to find decent remote data APIs to showcase. I seldom have the time or inclination to build my own, so I like to look for something interesting, amusing, or both.

If I simply ask ChatGPT to find me something, what will it provide me? I asked it to rewrite the service code to get data from a remote web server, without specifying what that server might be.

> Rewrite just that service code to get some sample data from a remote web server
>
> Certainly, let's modify the ApiService to retrieve some sample data from a publicly accessible API. In this case, we'll use the JSONPlaceholder API which is a simple fake REST API for testing and prototyping.
>
> Here's the updated service:
>
> ```
> import { Injectable } from '@angular/core';
> import { HttpClient } from '@angular/common/http';
> import { Observable } from 'rxjs';
> @Injectable({
>   providedIn: 'root'
> })
> export class ApiService {
>     private API_URL = 'https://jsonplaceholder.typicode.com/posts';
>   constructor(private http: HttpClient) { }
>   public getSampleData(): Observable<any> {
>     return this.http.get(this.API_URL);
>   }
> }
> ```

> In this version of the service, the getSampleData method will retrieve a list of sample posts from the JSONPlaceholder API.

That isn't what I expected, but it looks legitimate. So, I decided to try again with a different prompt.

> Add a function to get all posts from that API
>
> To get all posts from the JSONPlaceholder API, we can add a getAllPosts method to our ApiService. Here's how you can do that:
>
> ```
> import { Injectable } from '@angular/core';
> import { HttpClient } from '@angular/common/http';
> import { Observable } from 'rxjs';
> @Injectable({
>   providedIn: 'root'
> })
> export class ApiService {
>   private API_URL = 'https://jsonplaceholder.typicode.com';
>   constructor(private http: HttpClient) { }
>   public getAllPosts(): Observable<any> {
>     return this.http.get(`${this.API_URL}/posts`);
>   }
> }
> ```
>
> In this service, the getAllPosts method retrieves all posts from the JSONPlaceholder API.

That's pretty cool and as it turns out, that API is fully functional.

Let's Add Some RxJS

The call to `http.get` returns an Observable, but right now we aren't doing anything with it. What happens if we get an error? I decided to ask ChatGPT to modify `getAllPosts` to support error handling.

> Modify getAllPosts to support error handling
>
> Sure, to add error handling to the getAllPosts method, we can use the catchError operator from RxJS. This allows us to capture any errors that occur during the HTTP request and handle them appropriately.
>
> Here's how you might add error handling to the getAllPosts method:

```
import { Injectable } from '@angular/core';
import { HttpClient, HttpErrorResponse } from '@angular/common/http';
import { Observable, throwError } from 'rxjs';
import { catchError } from 'rxjs/operators';
@Injectable({
  providedIn: 'root'
})
export class ApiService {
  private API_URL = 'https://jsonplaceholder.typicode.com';
  constructor(private http: HttpClient) { }
  public getAllPosts(): Observable<any> {
    return this.http.get(`${this.API_URL}/posts`).pipe(
      catchError(this.handleError)
    );
  }
}
```

```
private handleError(error: HttpErrorResponse) {
  let errorMessage = 'Unknown error!';
  if (error.error instanceof ErrorEvent) {
    // Client-side errors
    errorMessage = `Error: ${error.error.message}`;
  } else {
    // Server-side errors
    errorMessage = `Error Code: ${error.status}\nMessage: ${error.message}`;
  }
  console.error(errorMessage);
  return throwError(errorMessage);
}
```

In this service, the handleError method is a private method that we use to handle any errors that occur during the HTTP request. We use this method in conjunction with the catchError operator to capture and handle any errors that occur.

Ok, that's exactly what I was expecting. Before I pressed Return, I was hoping it would suggest using `.pipe` and `.catchError`. That's exactly what it did. Adding the `handleError` function was above and beyond, which I appreciate.

Using the Observable in the Angular Template

What use is an Observable if we can't get its values?

The final example for this chapter is getting the posts from that API call onto a web page. I have to admit, this was pretty interesting.

I continued my conversation, so that it would remember the service it had already generated. One thing to realize when working with ChatGPT is that context is key. As long as you are in the same conversation, you should be able to refer back to what it's already built for you.

> Now I need an Angular Component where I can display these posts from the ApiService
>
> Sure, let's create a simple Angular component that retrieves posts from the ApiService and displays them.
>
> First, let's create the TypeScript file for the component:
>
> ```
> import { Component, OnInit } from '@angular/core';
> import { ApiService } from './api.service';
> @Component({
>   selector: 'app-posts',
>   templateUrl: './posts.component.html',
>   styleUrls: ['./posts.component.css']
> })
> export class PostsComponent implements OnInit {
>   posts: any[] = [];
>   constructor(private apiService: ApiService) { }
>   ngOnInit() {
>     this.apiService.getAllPosts().subscribe(
>       data => {
> ```

```
    this.posts = data;
  },
  error => {
    console.error('There was an error!', error);
  }
);
}
}
```

In this component, we're injecting ApiService and using it to fetch posts in the ngOnInit method. The fetched posts are then stored in the posts property.

Now let's create the corresponding HTML file for the component:

```
<div *ngIf="posts.length > 0; else noPosts">
  <h2>Posts</h2>
  <ul>
    <li *ngFor="let post of posts">
      <h3>{{ post.title }}</h3>
      <p>{{ post.body }}</p>
    </li>
  </ul>
</div>
<ng-template #noPosts>
  <p>No posts available.</p>
</ng-template>
```

In this template, we're using *ngIf to conditionally display the

> posts if there are any, otherwise we display a message saying "No posts available". We're using *ngFor to loop over the posts and display each one.
>
> This is a simple example and assumes that each post has title and body properties. You should adjust it according to the actual structure of the posts you're dealing with.

It correctly found and referenced the `ApiService` from the other file, including referencing the imports correctly. What it didn't do was offer the Angular CLI commands to create the files for me (hint: it will – just ask).

What about async pipes?

There is one beef I have with the code ChatGPT gave me. I prefer not to subscribe to Observables if I don't have to. Angular provides the `async` pipe, which automatically subscribes and unsubscribes as needed. Could I get it to handle that for me?

> Rewrite the component to use the async pipe instead of subscribing to the observable
>
> Certainly! The async pipe subscribes to an Observable or Promise and returns the latest value it has emitted. When a new value is emitted, the async pipe marks the component to be checked for changes.
>
> Here's how you can modify the PostsComponent to use the async pipe:
>
> ```
> import { Component, OnInit } from '@angular/core';
> import { Observable } from 'rxjs';
> import { ApiService } from './api.service';
> @Component({
> ```

```typescript
  selector: 'app-posts',
  templateUrl: './posts.component.html',
  styleUrls: ['./posts.component.css']
})
export class PostsComponent implements OnInit {
  posts$: Observable<any>;
  constructor(private apiService: ApiService) { }
  ngOnInit() {
    this.posts$ = this.apiService.getAllPosts();
  }
}
```

In this version of the component, posts$ is an Observable and we assign the Observable returned by getAllPosts to it.

And here's how you can modify the template to use the async pipe:

```html
<div *ngIf="(posts$ | async) as posts; else noPosts">
  <h2>Posts</h2>
  <ul>
    <li *ngFor="let post of posts">
      <h3>{{ post.title }}</h3>
      <p>{{ post.body }}</p>
    </li>
  </ul>
</div>
<ng-template #noPosts>
  <p>No posts available.</p>
```

> `</ng-template>`
>
> The async pipe subscribes to posts$ and assigns the emitted values to a local variable called posts. The rest of the template remains the same.
>
> Using the async pipe can simplify your code and help manage subscriptions. The async pipe automatically subscribes to the Observable when the component is created and unsubscribes when the component is destroyed, preventing potential memory leaks.

Overall, I was impressed with how well it did once I prompted it with the right hints.

Complete Example in a Single Prompt

You may be wondering whether it is always necessary to iterate over the code ChatGPT generates. Honestly, it's how I work best. I like to start with a simple prompt and then help it refine its answers for me.

However, as a test of ChatGPT's capabilities, I asked it to generate everything for me, using a single prompt. Here is the prompt and its complete output. I started a new conversation so that it wouldn't "remember" any of the code it had already written for me.

> Build me a complete angular service that fetches some sample data (perhaps blog posts) from a remote web service. Be sure to log any errors encountered. Then create a web page implemented as an angular component, which displays the blog post titles from the service in an unordered list. Prefer to use the angular async pipe in the template rather than subscribing to the observable.
>
> Sure, I'll create an Angular service and a component for you.
>
> Let's start with the Angular service. Let's assume the API

endpoint is `https://sampleapi.com/posts`. We will use the HttpClient to make a GET request to this endpoint.

```
import { Injectable } from '@angular/core';

import { HttpClient, HttpErrorResponse } from '@angular/common/http';

import { Observable, throwError } from 'rxjs';

import { catchError } from 'rxjs/operators';

export interface BlogPost {
  id: number;
  title: string;
  content: string;
  author: string;
}

@Injectable({
  providedIn: 'root',
})

export class BlogService {
  private postsUrl = 'https://sampleapi.com/posts';
  constructor(private http: HttpClient) {}
  getPosts(): Observable<BlogPost[]> {
   return this.http.get<BlogPost[]>(this.postsUrl).pipe(
    catchError(this.handleError)
   );
  }
  private handleError(error: HttpErrorResponse) {
   console.error(
```

```
      `Server returned code ${error.status}, ` +
    `body was: ${error.error}`
  );
    return throwError('Something bad happened; please try again later.');
  }
}
```

Now, let's create a component that uses the service to display the list of blog post titles.

```
import { Component, OnInit } from '@angular/core';
import { Observable } from 'rxjs';
import { BlogPost, BlogService } from './blog.service';
@Component({
  selector: 'app-blog-posts',
  template: `
    <ul>
      <li *ngFor="let post of posts$ | async">{{ post.title }}</li>
    </ul>
  `,
  styleUrls: ['./blog-posts.component.css']
})
export class BlogPostsComponent implements OnInit {
  posts$: Observable<BlogPost[]>;
  constructor(private blogService: BlogService) {}
  ngOnInit() {
    this.posts$ = this.blogService.getPosts();
```

```
}
}
```

In the `BlogPostsComponent`, we're injecting the `BlogService` in the constructor, and then we call `getPosts()` method in the `ngOnInit()` lifecycle hook to fetch the posts when the component is initialized. We're using the `async` pipe in the template to subscribe to the `Observable` returned by `getPosts()`, which will automatically update the view whenever a new value is emitted.

Please note that you need to import HttpClientModule in your AppModule to use HttpClient.

```
import { HttpClientModule } from '@angular/common/http';
@NgModule({
  declarations: [
    AppComponent,
    BlogPostsComponent
  ],
  imports: [
    BrowserModule,
    HttpClientModule
  ],
  providers: [],
  bootstrap: [AppComponent]
})
export class AppModule { }
```

Ensure to replace the URL with your actual API endpoint and modify the BlogPost interface to match the structure of your

> data.

Wow! ChatGPT built almost exactly the same code, complete with explanations. I said "almost" because it used a different API endpoint for this code and asked me to modify it manually. As I said, it no longer "remembered" any of the prior conversation.

My other complaint about what it wrote is that its information is slightly outdated. Angular 14.2 introduced a developer preview of "standalone components," which don't need to be contained inside an `NgModule`. You can even write entire applications without a single `NgModule`. Angular 15 officially made them part of the framework.

This is a minor thing, but it serves to illustrate an important point. ChatGPT's knowledge doesn't know much about the past 2 years. I asked ChatGPT to rewrite the above application with standalone components from Angular 15. This was its reply.

> Rewrite the above application with standalone components from Angular 15
>
> I'm sorry, but Angular 15 is not a version that exists - the latest version of Angular as of my knowledge cutoff date of September 2021 is Angular 12. However, I can provide an example of how to rewrite the application using Angular's componentless routes with the **ng-container** element, introduced in Angular 4.

It then proceeded to give me almost the same application as before but adding in some default routing. Angular 12 is 4 versions old as I write this. It is not even supported anymore.

> *Let this be a friendly reminder and warning. ChatGPT is amazing at what it does, if you're looking for information that tends to be long-lived.*

That's why it does so well with regular expressions, scripting, and common algorithms. By its own admission, its knowledge can be woefully outdated, especially in this industry, which moves as fast as it does.

REGULAR EXPRESSIONS

Image by Author and OpenAI

Input validation is a critical component of ensuring data integrity and preventing security vulnerabilities. However, crafting effective regular expressions (regexes) can be a time-consuming and challenging task. That's where ChatGPT comes in. In this chapter, I set out to explore how well they could generate regexes for input validation using nothing more than a simple prompt in the form of a comment. Read on to discover my findings and the surprising effectiveness of this AI-powered tool.

Regex 101 Site

I decided to use an existing regex website to help me test what ChatGPT provided: regex101: build, test, and debug regex. (https://regex101.com)

This site lets me choose what type of regular expression to test and has some really cool error detection and debugging features.

Email Address

The first thing that came to mind is evaluating a string to see if it is a valid email address.

> Give me a regular expression to validate an email address
>
> `^[a-zA-Z0-9._%+-]+@[a-zA-Z0-9.-]+\.[a-zA-Z]{2,}$`

ChatGPT provided a lengthy explanation of the regex it gave me, which I won't reproduce here. Suffice it to say that it was complete. More importantly, how does it work on the data?

Matched

mike@company.com
mike@company.co.uk
x@y.com
mike@x.cc

Not Matched

mike@localhost
mike@10.0.0.1
mike@x.
Bill

It missed the two valid emails with localhost and an IP address as the domain. Technically, those are valid. So, it's not bad, but I'm wondering how it stacks up to the professionals.

According to a an article I found on the most

comprehensive email regex, this is "the best" email pattern:

```
([-!#-'*+/-9=?A-Z^-~]+(\.[-!#-'*+/-9=?A-Z^-~]+)*|"([]!#-[^-~ \t]|(\\
[\t   -~]))+")@([0-9A-Za-z]([0-9A-Za-z-]{0,61}[0-9A-Za-z])?(\.
[0-9A-Za-z]([0-9A-Za-z-]{0,61}[0-9A-Za-z])?)*|\[(((25[0-5]|2[0-4]
[0-9]|1[0-9]{2}|[1-9]?[0-9])(\.(25[0-5]|2[0-4][0-9]|1[0-9]{2}|
[1-9]?[0-9])){3}|IPv6:(((((0|[1-9A-Fa-f][0-9A-Fa-f]{0,3}):){6}|::((0|
[1-9A-Fa-f][0-9A-Fa-f]{0,3}):){5}|[0-9A-Fa-f]{0,4}::((0|[1-9A-Fa-
f][0-9A-Fa-f]{0,3}):){4}|(((0|[1-9A-Fa-f][0-9A-Fa-f]{0,3}):)?(0|
[1-9A-Fa-f][0-9A-Fa-f]{0,3}))?::((0|[1-9A-Fa-f][0-9A-Fa-f]
{0,3}):){3}|(((0|[1-9A-Fa-f][0-9A-Fa-f]{0,3}):){0,2}(0|[1-9A-Fa-f]
[0-9A-Fa-f]{0,3}))?::((0|[1-9A-Fa-f][0-9A-Fa-f]{0,3}):){2}|(((0|
[1-9A-Fa-f][0-9A-Fa-f]{0,3}):){0,3}(0|[1-9A-Fa-f][0-9A-Fa-f]
{0,3}))?::(0|[1-9A-Fa-f][0-9A-Fa-f]{0,3}):|(((0|[1-9A-Fa-f][0-9A-
Fa-f]{0,3}):){0,4}(0|[1-9A-Fa-f][0-9A-Fa-f]{0,3}))?::)((0|[1-9A-
Fa-f][0-9A-Fa-f]{0,3}):(0|[1-9A-Fa-f][0-9A-Fa-f]{0,3})|(25[0-5]|
2[0-4][0-9]|1[0-9]{2}|[1-9]?[0-9])(\.(25[0-5]|2[0-4][0-9]|1[0-9]
{2}|[1-9]?[0-9])){3})|(((0|[1-9A-Fa-f][0-9A-Fa-f]{0,3}):){0,5}(0|
[1-9A-Fa-f][0-9A-Fa-f]{0,3}))?::(0|[1-9A-Fa-f][0-9A-Fa-f]{0,3})|
(((0|[1-9A-Fa-f][0-9A-Fa-f]{0,3}):){0,6}(0|[1-9A-Fa-f][0-9A-Fa-f]
{0,3}))?::)|(?!IPv6:)[0-9A-Za-z-]*[0-9A-Za-z]:[!-Z^-~]+)])
```

That's a 1240-character regex! It looks nothing like the one the AI gave me.

This one did much better, including matching two valid email addresses from the above list that the first regex did not.

mike@localhost
mike@10.0.0.1

Honestly, I think that both regexes from the are fine, but ChatGPT's did miss those two valid email addresses.

Phone numbers

Moving on, how well will it do validating a phone number? I gave it a prompt to see what it came up with:

> Give me a regex that can validate any phone number, us or international, liberally accepting common punctuation.

```
/^(\+\d{1,4}[-.\s])?(\()?(\d{1,4})?(\))?[-.\s]?(\d{1,4})[-.\s]?(\d{1,9})$/
```

It didn't do very well, matching only the first two UK numbers, and failing others I would hope would be matched.

Matched
2025551212
8002822882
603 555 1212
(603) 555 1212
+01 202 555 1212
+44 889 234 1239
+44.889.234.1239

Not matched
+12025551212
+14079393463
603–555–1212
+014079393463
+44 889–234–1239
(202) 555–1212
800–282–2882

Before I give up, consider that it might be a matter of telling ChatGPT what your expectations are. Why not give it some of your sample data? Consider this

prompt and its response:

> The regex you provided only matched half of my data set. The sample data is as follows:
>
> Matched
>
> 2025551212
>
> 8002822882
>
> 603 555 1212
>
> (603) 555 1212
>
> +01 202 555 1212
>
> +44 889 234 1239
>
> +44.889.234.1239
>
> Not matched
>
> +12025551212
>
> +14079393463
>
> 603–555–1212
>
> +014079393463
>
> +44 889–234–1239
>
> (202) 555–1212
>
> 800–282–2882
>
> They should all match. Generate a new regex.
>
> To match all the examples you provided, you can use a regular expression that takes into account variations in digit separators. The separators can be a space, a dot, a dash, or none at all. Here's a regex pattern that should work:
>
> `/^(\+\d{1,2}\s?)?((\()?\d{3}(\))?[\s.-]?)?\d{3}[\s.-]?\d{4}$/`

Here's a breakdown of the pattern:

- `^` - Start of the string.
- `(\+\d{1,2}\s?)?` - Matches zero or one occurrence of a plus sign followed by one or two digits and an optional space (for the international dialing code).
- `((\()?\d{3}(\))?[\s.-]?)?` - Matches zero or one occurrence of an optional opening parenthesis, three digits, an optional closing parenthesis, and an optional space, dot, or dash (for the area code).
- `\d{3}[\s.-]?` - Matches three digits followed by an optional space, dot, or dash.
- `\d{4}` - Matches the last four digits.
- `$` - End of the string.

Here's how you can use this pattern in JavaScript:

```
let phoneNumbers = [
"2025551212",
"8002822882",
"603 555 1212",
"+01 202 555 1212",
"+44 889 234 1239",
"+44.889.234.1239",
"+12025551212",
"+14079393463",
"603-555-1212",
"+014079393463",
"+44 889-234-1239",
"(202) 555-1212",
```

```
  "800-282-2882"
];
let pattern = /^(\+\d{1,2}\s?)?((\()?\d{3}(\))?[\s.-]?)?\d{3}[\s.-]?\d{4}$/;
for (let phoneNumber of phoneNumbers) {
  if(pattern.test(phoneNumber)) {
    console.log(phoneNumber + " matches");
  } else {
    console.log(phoneNumber + " does not match");
  }
}
```

This script will log whether each phone number in the array matches the regex pattern.

Remember that this pattern will not check whether the phone number is a valid phone number, only whether it matches the expected pattern. Always handle phone numbers securely and in compliance with all relevant privacy laws and regulations.

What do you think? Are you convinced? I admit it is very convincing and authoritative. And it did do a better job matching my sample dataset. It still neglected to match five of them, though.

Matched
2025551212
8002822882
603 555 1212
(603) 555 1212
+01 202 555 1212
+44 889 234 1239

+12025551212
+14079393463
+014079393463

Not matched

603-555-1212
+44.889.234.1239
+44 889-234-1239
(202) 555-1212
800-282-2882

Or perhaps matching a phone number is simply too difficult with a regex. I guess this is why most websites use a masked input to accept phone numbers.

Valid URL

Related to, though not specifically about validation, I wanted to see whether it would give me a pattern to recognize valid all URLs inside a string. That could be useful for crawling websites. As with the rest of the examples, I started with a prompt.

ChatGPT took me literally, as it has been doing throughout all my research and experimentation.

> Give me a regex to find all URLs from img and a tags in the text of an HTML page.
>
> `/<(img|a)\b[^>]*?\b(src|href)\s*=\s*["']?([^"'>\s]*)/gi`

It did not give me a regex looking to match URLs. Instead, it is a regex that extracts the entire string inside the quotes following an `img` or `href` attribute. That is, in fact, exactly what I asked for.

Not wanting to give up just yet, I offered a

more explicit prompt to ChatGPT to tweak its understanding.

> Give me a regex matching URLs found in an arbitrary document of text, which may or may not be HTML.
>
> Matching URLs with a regular expression can be complex, as there are many valid forms a URL can take. Here's a relatively simple pattern that should match most common URLs:
>
> ```
> \b((http|https):\/\/)?([\w-]+\.)+[\w-]+(\/[\w- ;,./?%&=]*)?
> ```
>
> Here's a breakdown of the pattern:
>
> \b - Asserts a word boundary.
>
> ((http|https):\/\/)? - Matches "http://" or "https://" at the beginning of the URL, if present.
>
> ([\w-]+\.)+[\w-]+ - Matches one or more word characters (a-z, A-Z, 0-9, or _) or hyphens, followed by a period, one or more times. Then matches one or more word characters or hyphens. This should match the domain and top-level domain of the URL.
>
> (\/[\w- ;,./?%&=]*)? - Optionally matches a slash followed by zero or more word characters, hyphens, spaces, semicolons, commas, periods, slashes, question marks, percent signs, ampersands, equals signs, or underscores. This should match the path and query string of the URL, if present.
>
> Here's an example of how to use this pattern in JavaScript:
>
> ```
> let text = "Visit https://www.example.com or http://example.com/page?query=test for more info.";
> let pattern = /\b((http|https):\/\/)?([\w-]+\.)+[\w-]+(\/[\w- ;,./?%&=]*)?/g;
> let match;
> while ((match = pattern.exec(text)) !== null) {
> ```

```
console.log(match[0]);
}
```

This script will log any URLs found in the input string. This pattern isn't perfect and may not match all possible URLs, but it should work for most common cases. It's also worth noting that this pattern does not validate URLs - it just matches patterns that look like URLs.

As you can see, its explanation was comprehensive; it even gave me sample code to show me how to call it. I tested what it offered and discovered that it was by far the best regular expression.

This would be a better regex to use if you were validating that a given string is, in fact, a URL.

Password complexity

Just about every web site that lets users register has some rule about password complexity. Can it generate a regex to validate such passwords?

> Give me a regex to validate password complexity with the following rules: Passwords much contain at least one number, one lowercase and one uppercase letter, one symbol, and be 8 characters or longer.

You can use positive lookaheads in your regular expression to ensure the password meets all the given requirements. Here is a regex for this:

```
/^(?=.*\d)(?=.*[a-z])(?=.*[A-Z])(?=.*[\W_]).{8,}$/
```

This pattern can be broken down as follows:

- `^` - Start of the string.

- `(?=.*\d)` - Positive lookahead to assert that there is at least one digit.

- `(?=.*[a-z])` - Positive lookahead to assert that there is at least one lowercase letter.

- `(?=.*[A-Z])` - Positive lookahead to assert that there is at least one uppercase letter.

- `(?=.*[\W_])` - Positive lookahead to assert that there is at least one non-word character (any character not a-z, A-Z, 0-9) or underscore. This covers your requirement for a symbol.

- `.{8,}` - Matches any character (except newline) 8 times or more.

- `$` - End of the string.

That's quite the regex, but is it correct? Back over at regex101.com, I put it to the test. Here is how it did with my sample passwords:

Valid Passwords
P@55word
This1s@GoodPassword
MikeWasHerein1999!

Invalid Passwords
password
MikeWasHere!
This is a bad password
12345

My hastily-considered opinion is that this is a good regex for its purpose.

Valid U.S. currency

Another common scenario is determining whether or not input is valid US currency.

> Give me a regex that will validate that the input is a US currency

A regex pattern that validates US currency, including optional cents and optional thousands separators, could be something like:

```
/^\$?(\d{1,3}(\,\d{3})*|(\d+))(\.\d{2})?$/
```

Here's a breakdown of this pattern:

^\$? - Matches an optional dollar sign at the beginning of the string.

(\d{1,3}(\,\d{3})*|(\d+)) - Matches either a number with optional comma separators every three digits or a number without any comma separators.

(\.\d{2})? - Matches an optional decimal point followed by exactly two digits (for cents).

$ - End of the string. Ensures that the whole string must match the pattern (not just a part of it).

This one looks good at first glance. I tried a short list of strings that I imagine people might enter into a web page as currency. Let's see how that regex did.

Valid Currency

$1
0.79
1.49
$0.00
$0.43
$1,230,847,369.99

Invalid Currency

Mike
.22
$.25
1.575

1.57$
2.25%
1 dollar

Looks pretty good to me except for the .22 and $.25. I'd call that a partial pass. As we have previously seen, a cool thing you can do with ChatGPT is give it additional examples and ask it to fix its prior answers.

> Modify that regex to match currency like .22 and $.25 also
>
> If you want to include cases where the amount can start with a decimal point, you can modify the regex to the following:
>
> ```
> /^\$?((\d{1,3}(\,\d{3})*|(\d+))(\.\d{2})?|(\.\d{2}))$/
> ```
>
> Here's a breakdown of the changes:
>
> ^\$? - Matches an optional dollar sign at the beginning of the string.
>
> ((\d{1,3}(\,\d{3})*|(\d+))(\.\d{2})?|(\.\d{2})) - Matches either a number with optional comma separators every three digits, a number without any comma separators, or a number that starts with a decimal point. All may be followed by an optional decimal point and exactly two digits (for cents).
>
> $ - End of the string. Ensures that the whole string must match the pattern (not just a part of it).

And just like that, we have a much better regular expression than we would have otherwise. In fact, if you know roughly what kinds of values you want to be able to accept, you can provide them all in a single prompt. ChatGPT will most likely do the right thing for you.

> Given a potential list of different ways to write US currency, write a regular expression that will match all of these: $1 .22 $.25 0.79 1.49 $0.00 $0.43 $1,230,847,369.99

> Here's a regular expression that can match all of the given examples of US currency values:
>
> ```
> ^(?:\$\s?)?(?:\d{1,3}(?:,\d{3})*|\d+)(?:\.\d{2})?$
> ```
>
> Let's break down this regular expression:
>
> ^ - Start of the line
>
> (?:\$\s?)? - Optionally match a dollar sign followed by an optional whitespace character
>
> (?:\d{1,3}(?:,\d{3})*|\d+) - Match either a sequence of 1-3 digits, optionally followed by groups of three digits separated by commas, or a single sequence of one or more digits.
>
> (?:\.\d{2})? - Optionally match a period followed by exactly two digits
>
> $ - End of the line
>
> This regular expression matches the given examples of US currency values, including dollar amounts with or without the dollar sign, decimal points and commas.
>
> Note that this regular expression does not match negative amounts. Also, if you have currency values with unusual formats, such as negative amounts or amounts with more than two decimal places, you may need to modify the regular expression accordingly.

How well do you think it did?

It got all of them except the $.25 value. Not bad, but it shows that ChatGPT isn't infallible. However, I do appreciate the power of giving it examples and letting it do the rest.

U.S. Social Security Number

What about social security numbers? Those are pretty straightforward in the US, so I didn't expect too much of a challenge here.

> Write a regex that will validate that the input is a valid SSN.
>
> A regex pattern for validating U.S. Social Security numbers (SSNs), which are formatted as "XXX-XX-XXXX" where each X is a digit, can be:
>
> ```
> /^\d{3}-\d{2}-\d{4}$/
> ```
>
> Here's a breakdown of this pattern:
>
> ^ - Start of the string.
>
> \d{3} - Exactly three digits.
>
> - - A hyphen.
>
> \d{2} - Exactly two digits.
>
> - - A hyphen.
>
> \d{4} - Exactly four digits.
>
> $ - End of the string.

Valid SSN

999-99-9999

012-34-5678

978-76-5432

Invalid SSN

978 76 5432

97-876-5432

5432-76-978

xxx-yy-zzzz

Valid credit card numbers

I expected that this one might pose a little more of a challenge. Validating credit card numbers is a common task for web apps. However, relying solely on regular expressions (regex) to validate credit card numbers can be dangerous. While regex is a powerful tool for pattern matching, it may not catch all potential errors or security risks associated with credit card numbers.

This is because credit card numbers have a complex structure with multiple rules and restrictions, and regex patterns may not always account for all of them. Credit card numbers are not simply a pattern of grouped digits, though they may appear to be at first glance. I don't think a regex can compute the checksum (aka Luhn Algorithm), so I think we may have to settle for "close."

Apparently, though, ChatGPT is also aware of these limitations, as you will see.

> Validate a credit card number

Validating a credit card number involves more than just a regular expression. Credit card numbers have specific characteristics depending on the issuing network, and they also include a check digit that is calculated using the Luhn algorithm.

However, a regular expression can be used for a basic format check. Here's a simple regex that checks if the input consists of 13 to 19 digits, which is the usual range for credit card numbers:

```
/^\d{13,19}$/
```

If you want to validate a credit card number more thoroughly, you could use the Luhn algorithm. Here's an example of how to do that in JavaScript:

```
function validateCardNumber(number) {
```

```javascript
  let regex = new RegExp("^[0-9]{13,19}$");
  if (!regex.test(number)) return false;
  let sum = 0;
  for (let i = 0; i < number.length; i++) {
    let digit = parseInt(number[number.length - 1 - i]);
    if (i % 2 === 1) {
      digit *= 2;
      if (digit > 9) {
        digit -= 9;
      }
    }
    sum += digit;
  }
  return sum % 10 === 0;
}
console.log(validateCardNumber("1234567890123456")); // Replace with the card number
```

The `validateCardNumber` function first checks if the input matches the regex, and then it calculates the Luhn checksum. The card number is valid if the checksum modulo 10 is equal to 0.

Please note that these are simple validation checks and won't verify if a credit card number is actually active or genuine. Always handle credit card numbers securely and in compliance with all relevant laws and regulations, such as the Payment Card Industry Data Security Standard (PCI DSS).

The regex might be good for a first-pass client-side validation, but it's far from perfect. Naturally, you'll want to rely on your payment processor for additional validation. Better yet, don't roll your own credit card processing!

HTML tags

Can ChatGPT recognize legal HTML tags in a body of text?

> Write a regex to recognize all HTML tags in the input text.
>
> To recognize all HTML tags in a given input, you can use the following regular expression:
>
> ```
> /<\/?[a-z][\w-]*(?:\s+[a-z_-]+(?:\s*=\s*(?:"[^"]*"|'[^']*'|[^>\s]+))?)*\s*\/?>/gi
> ```
>
> Here's a breakdown of this pattern:
>
> - `<` - Matches the beginning of an HTML tag.
>
> - `\/?` - Matches zero or one forward slash, which would indicate a closing tag.
>
> - `[a-z][\w-]*` - Matches an HTML tag name, which should start with a letter and can be followed by any number of word characters or hyphens.
>
> - `(?:\s+[a-z_-]+(?:\s*=\s*(?:"[^"]*"|'[^']*'|[^>\s]+))?)*` - Matches any number of HTML attributes. An attribute consists of some whitespace, followed by the attribute name, and optionally an equals sign and the attribute value. The value can be enclosed in double quotes, single quotes, or not enclosed at all.
>
> - `\s*` - Matches any amount of whitespace.
>
> - `\/?` - Matches zero or one forward slash, which would indicate a self-closing tag.
>
> - `>` - Matches the end of an HTML tag.
>
> - `gi` - The `g` flag makes this a global search, so it will find all matches in the input string, not just the first one. The `i` flag

makes the search case-insensitive.

Please note that parsing HTML with regex can be error-prone, especially for complex HTML. For robust HTML parsing or manipulation, consider using an HTML parsing library instead.

Detect Repeated Words

How hard would it be to detect repeated words in a piece of text?

Find repeated words in the input text

You can use a regular expression to find repeated words in a text. Here's a simple pattern that should match most common cases:

`/\b(\w+)\b(?=.*\b\1\b)/g`

Here's a breakdown of the pattern:

- `\b` - Word boundary. This prevents the pattern from matching words that merely contain the repeated word.

- `(\w+)` - Matches one or more word characters (a-z, A-Z, 0-9, or _) and captures them into group 1. This is the word we're checking for repeats of.

- `\b` - Another word boundary.

- `(?=.*\b\1\b)` - Positive lookahead. This checks that another instance of the word captured in group 1 appears somewhere later in the string. The `\b` word boundaries ensure we're matching the whole word, not a word that happens to contain the repeated word.

- `/g` - Global flag. This allows the pattern to find all repeated words, not just the first one.

Also, this regex is case-sensitive. If you want to ignore case, you can add the `i` flag to the regex (`/pattern/gi`).

I expected this one to be more complicated than it was, but on reflection, this is the kind of thing regular expressions really good for

Valid JavaScript identifiers

This one made sense after I saw what it wrote, but it wasn't what I expected (honestly, I'm not sure what I expected).

> Recognize all valid JavaScript keywords in the input text
>
> JavaScript has a number of reserved keywords which you can recognize using a regular expression. As of my knowledge cut-off in September 2021, the reserved keywords are:
>
> await, break, case, catch, class, const, continue, debugger, default, delete, do, else, enum, export, extends, false, finally, for, function, if, implements, import, in, instanceof, interface, let, new, null, package, private, protected, public, return, super, switch, this, throw, true, try, typeof, var, void, while, with, yield
>
> However, recognizing keywords in arbitrary text can be tricky. If you're looking to simply find occurrences of these keywords in a text, you can use a regular expression like this:
>
> /\b(await|break|case|catch|class|const|continue|debugger|default|delete|do|else|enum|export|extends|false|finally|for|function|if|implements|import|in|instanceof|interface|let|new|null|package|private|protected|public|return|super|switch|this|throw|true|try|typeof|var|void|while|with|yield)\b/g
>
> Please note that this does not validate the usage of these keywords in actual JavaScript code. It will simply match these keywords wherever they appear in the text. If you want to perform actual JavaScript code validation, you would need to use a JavaScript parser or linter.

Conclusion

As I hope you will agree, I think it's safe to say that ChatGPT *can help* with regular expressions.

As with any code written for you by an AI (or even other developers), you can't simply accept what you're given without question. It's important to understand what the code does.

As I have written previously, I will continue to use it where it makes sense. I will not, however, blindly use everything written for me by an AI.

DATA GENERATION

Image by Thorsten Frenzel from Pixabay

Never Lack Sample Data for Your Apps

Generating sample data is a crucial aspect of application development, as it allows developers to test and refine their software in a controlled environment. In this chapter, we will explore the effectiveness of ChatGPT in generating sample data for applications. We will start with simple examples and gradually move towards more complex ideas, sharing both the successes and failures along the way. By the end of this chapter, you will have a better understanding of the capabilities and limitations of these tools and how they can be leveraged to improve your application development process.

As before I will show my simple comment, followed by what the AIs suggested, with commentary where appropriate.

Lorem Ipsum Text

I do a lot of UI development. Early in the app creation process, I like it when my pages appear to have content. I often turn to "lorem ipsum" text, which is nonsense text that has the same general "look and feel" of English when rendered on the page. There are dedicated websites that will generate it, but I thought it might be nice to have ChatGPT do it instead.

> Generate a paragraph of lorem ipsum text
>
> Lorem ipsum dolor sit amet, consectetur adipiscing elit. Vestibulum dignissim sagittis sapien, sed cursus erat condimentum nec. Pellentesque habitant morbi tristique senectus et netus et malesuada fames ac turpis egestas. Mauris ultrices augue ac metus fermentum, ac efficitur mauris pharetra. Vivamus egestas arcu lacus, in vulputate augue fringilla a. Donec rutrum, felis eu facilisis mollis, justo risus pulvinar mi, at aliquam ante sem in nunc. Integer ornare, est et lacinia tincidunt, arcu nulla ultrices ligula, in pharetra diam tellus et nisl.

It did exactly what I expected without any additional explanation. It just worked.

List of schools in the USA

For the next experiment, I wanted a list of schools that can be found in the United States. ChatGPT again came through.

Give me a list of schools in the USA as a JavaScript array

Sure, here's an example of how you might create a JavaScript array of schools in the USA. Please note that this is just a very small selection of schools for illustrative purposes:

```
var schoolsInUSA = [
    {name: "Harvard University", city: "Cambridge", state: "Massachusetts"},
    {name: "Stanford University", city: "Stanford", state: "California"},
    {name: "Yale University", city: "New Haven", state: "Connecticut"},
    {name: "Massachusetts Institute of Technology", city: "Cambridge", state: "Massachusetts"},
  {name: "California Institute of Technology", city: "Pasadena", state: "California"},
    {name: "University of Chicago", city: "Chicago", state: "Illinois"},
   {name: "Princeton University", city: "Princeton", state: "New Jersey"},
    {name: "Columbia University", city: "New York", state: "New York"},
    {name: "University of Pennsylvania", city: "Philadelphia", state: "Pennsylvania"},
    {name: "Duke University", city: "Durham", state: "North Carolina"}
];
```

This array contains objects, each representing a different school. Each object has `name`, `city`, and `state` properties. This is a common format for organizing data in

JavaScript.

Fake Customers with Addresses

Next, could it generate some fake customers for me? Given what you've already seen, you probably have reasonable faith in ChatGPT getting this right.

> Generate a list of random customer names and addresses

> For the purpose of privacy and data protection, it's not appropriate to provide real customer names and addresses. However, I can generate a list of fictional customer names and addresses for you. Here it is:

```
var customers = [
    {name: "John Doe", address: "123 Main St, Springfield, IL 62704"},
    {name: "Jane Smith", address: "456 Oak St, Bakersfield, CA 93304"},
    {name: "Alice Johnson", address: "789 Pine St, Boulder, CO 80302"},
    {name: "Robert Brown", address: "321 Elm St, Tulsa, OK 74103"},
    {name: "Mary Davis", address: "654 Maple St, Topeka, KS 66603"},
    {name: "James Miller", address: "987 Cedar St, Reno, NV 89501"},
    {name: "Patricia Wilson", address: "345 Spruce St, Biloxi, MS 39530"},
    {name: "Richard Taylor", address: "678 Walnut St, Fargo, ND 58102"},
    {name: "Jennifer Moore", address: "901 Birch St, Bangor, ME
```

> 04401"},
>
> {name: "Charles White", address: "234 Poplar St, Helena, MT 59601"}
>
>];
>
> Please note that these names and addresses are completely made up and any resemblance to real locations is purely coincidental.

Random Color generation

Have you ever needed some random colors? I admit this one is a bit less impressive, but I was determined to continue. ChatGPT took my comment and rewrote its entire code block, adding the new functionality where appropriate. Here are the relevant lines it added:

> Add a random color to each customer
>
> Sure, let's add a `favoriteColor` property to each customer. I'll use a small list of colors for simplicity:
>
> var customers = [
>
> {name: "John Doe", address: "123 Main St, Springfield, IL 62704", favoriteColor: "Red"},
>
> {name: "Jane Smith", address: "456 Oak St, Bakersfield, CA 93304", favoriteColor: "Blue"},
>
> {name: "Alice Johnson", address: "789 Pine St, Boulder, CO 80302", favoriteColor: "Green"},
>
> {name: "Robert Brown", address: "321 Elm St, Tulsa, OK 74103", favoriteColor: "Yellow"},
>
> {name: "Mary Davis", address: "654 Maple St, Topeka, KS 66603", favoriteColor: "Purple"},

```
    {name: "James Miller", address: "987 Cedar St, Reno, NV
89501", favoriteColor: "Orange"},

    {name: "Patricia Wilson", address: "345 Spruce St, Biloxi, MS
39530", favoriteColor: "Pink"},

    {name: "Richard Taylor", address: "678 Walnut St, Fargo, ND
58102", favoriteColor: "Brown"},

    {name: "Jennifer Moore", address: "901 Birch St, Bangor, ME
04401", favoriteColor: "Black"},

    {name: "Charles White", address: "234 Poplar St, Helena, MT
59601", favoriteColor: "White"}
];
```

Again, this is just an illustrative example. In a real situation, you would probably want to generate the colors randomly or based on some other criteria.

Would it do as well if I asked it to use CSS colors? It did so, though not exactly the way I expected. It decided that I wanted to add the CSS colors in addition to the named colors. It also made sure that the CSS color values matched the named colors. What I wanted, instead, was to replace the named color with a random CSS value.

The cool thing, as I will continue to stress, is that you can simply ask it regenerate it. I won't show you the entire code block, just one of the customers.

Regenerate that, replacing the favoriteColor with a random CSS color value instead.

Sure, here's the updated JavaScript array with `favoriteColor` replaced by random CSS color codes:

```
var customers = [
```

```
{
    name: "John Doe",
    address: "123 Main St, Springfield, IL 62704",
    favoriteColor: "#FF6347"
},
...
];
```

Please note that these CSS color values are not truly random, but have been selected for variety. In a real application, you might want to use a function to generate truly random color codes.

Code Formatting

If you are frustrated at all by the formatting of the code blocks so far, know that you aren't alone. However, I asked ChatGPT to fix that, using the following prompt.

> From this point on, pretty-format any code you output, wrapping at 60 characters

Sure, here's the previous JavaScript array formatted to wrap at 60 characters:

... code omitted ...

This format makes the code easier to read, especially when dealing with more complex objects.

Movie titles

What about movie titles? Would it be able to generate real movies or real-sounding fake movies? ChatGPT did exactly what I had hoped it would do from the beginning. Again, I'll only show you a little of the data it generated.

> Add a favorite movie to each customer
>
> Sure, let's add a `favoriteMovie` property to each customer. I'll use a small list of popular movies for simplicity:
>
> ```
> var customers = [
>   {
>     name: "John Doe",
>     address: "123 Main St, Springfield, IL 62704",
>     favoriteColor: "#FF6347",
>     favoriteMovie: "Star Wars"
>   },
>   {
>     name: "Jane Smith",
>     address: "456 Oak St, Bakersfield, CA 93304",
>     favoriteColor: "#8A2BE2",
>     favoriteMovie: "The Godfather"
>   },
>   ...
> ];
> ```
>
> Again, this is just an illustrative example. In a real situation, you would probably want to generate the movies randomly or based on some other criteria.

Given the movie list, my expectations for ChatGPT were still pretty high that it could tackle the rest of my list of sample data. I will present the rest of them here without comment unless the results were out of line with my expectations.

Car Makes and Models

```
What kind of car does each customer drive?
var customers = [
  {
    name: "John Doe",
    address: "123 Main St, Springfield, IL 62704",
    favoriteColor: "#FF6347",
    favoriteMovie: "Star Wars",
    car: "Toyota Camry"
  },
  ...
```

Dog breeds

ChatGPT

```
What kind of dog does each customer have?
var customers = [
  {
    name: "John Doe",
    address: "123 Main St, Springfield, IL 62704",
    favoriteColor: "#FF6347",
    favoriteMovie: "Star Wars",
    car: "Toyota Camry",
    dog: "Golden Retriever"
```

```
},
...
```

Deck of cards

I wasn't sure about this one. Some of the other Ais I have tried didn't do so well, but I had high hopes for ChatGPT figuring it out.

Create an array of all possible card values

Sure, here's how you can generate a deck of cards in JavaScript:

```
function createDeck() {
  const suits = ['Hearts', 'Diamonds', 'Clubs', 'Spades'];
   const values = ['2', '3', '4', '5', '6', '7', '8', '9', '10', 'Jack', 'Queen', 'King', 'Ace'];
  let deck = [];
  for (let suit of suits) {
    for (let value of values) {
      deck.push({
        suit: suit,
        value: value
      });
    }
  }
  return deck;
}
let deck = createDeck();
// Shuffle the deck
```

```
deck.sort(() => Math.random() - 0.5);
```

```
console.log(deck);
```

This code first creates an ordered deck of cards, and then shuffles it using a simple random sort. Each card is represented as an object with a `suit` and a `value` property.

Apparently, it forgot about my request to wrap at 60 characters. I'll fix that on my next prompt. Consider it a reminder that sometimes you have to ask more than once.

When I asked it to shuffle the deck, I expected it to use built-in array functions, but it did not. Instead, it wrote a shuffle function the hard way.

Give me a function to shuffle the deck, and please remember my request to wrap at 60 characters to make formatting prettier.

Absolutely, here is a JavaScript function that uses the Fisher-Yates (also known as Knuth) shuffle algorithm to shuffle a deck of cards... wrapped at approximately 60 characters for better readability:

```
function shuffleDeck(deck) {
  for (let i = deck.length - 1; i > 0; i--) {
    let j = Math.floor(Math.random() * (i + 1));
    [deck[i], deck[j]] = [deck[j], deck[i]];
  }
  return deck;
}
```

You can use this function to shuffle your deck of cards by calling `shuffleDeck(deck)`. This function works by iterating over the array from the last element to the first, choosing a random index less than or equal to the current index, and swapping the elements at the current index and the random index. This ensures that every permutation of the deck is equally likely.

Encouraged by its understanding, however, I asked it one more time, this time instructing it to use built-in array functions.

> Rewrite that function to shuffle the deck using built-in JavaScript array functionality
>
> Sure, you can also shuffle an array in JavaScript using built-in functions. Here is a function using the `sort` method with a random comparator:
>
> ```
> function shuffleDeck(deck) {
>   return deck.sort(() => Math.random() - 0.5);
> }
> ```
>
> This method is simple, but it's worth noting that it doesn't provide a perfectly uniform distribution of shuffle outcomes. If you need a truly random shuffle, the Fisher-Yates method mentioned earlier is recommended.

That should do the trick. It's all about asking for exactly what you want. Unfortunately, it also told me that I was wrong, which is interesting feedback. Maybe there is a good reason it offers the code it does. The nice thing about ChatGPT is that you can always ask for a more thorough explanation.

> Would you explain that last comment about Fisher-Yates so that I understand the issue, please?
>
> Sure, I'd be happy to explain.
>
> The `.sort()` method with a random comparator function is

often used for its simplicity and brevity. However, it doesn't provide a uniform distribution of shuffles. In other words, some arrangements of the deck are more likely to occur than others, which isn't ideal when you're trying to shuffle a deck of cards.

The reason for this is subtle: The `.sort()` function in JavaScript (and in many other languages) is not designed to work correctly with comparators that return inconsistent results. A correct comparator for `.sort()` should always return the same result when given the same two elements, regardless of their current order or position in the array. But the random comparator we're using doesn't do this—it can return different results each time it's called with the same two elements. This can cause the `.sort()` function to behave unpredictably.

On the other hand, the Fisher-Yates (or Knuth) shuffle algorithm is designed to provide a uniform distribution. It works by iterating through the array from the last element to the first, and for each element, swapping it with an element at a random index less than or equal to the current one. This ensures that every possible permutation of the deck is equally likely.

For a deck of cards or any other application where a fair shuffle is important, the Fisher-Yates shuffle is generally the better choice.

Now that's showing your work!

Deck of uno cards

Do you think ChatGPT even knows what Uno cards are?

Create a random deck of Uno cards

Creating a deck of UNO cards involves a bit more complexity

than a standard deck of cards, as UNO cards have multiple types and colors. Here's an example of how you can generate a deck of UNO cards:

```javascript
function createUnoDeck() {
  const colors = ['Red', 'Green', 'Blue', 'Yellow'];
  const values = [
    '0', '1', '2', '3', '4', '5', '6',
    '7', '8', '9', 'Skip', 'Reverse',
    'Draw Two'
  ];
  const wilds = ['Wild', 'Wild Draw Four'];
  let deck = [];
  for (let color of colors) {
    for (let value of values) {
      let card = {
        color: color,
        value: value
      };
      deck.push(card);
      // Add two of each card in each
      // color, except for 0
      if (value !== '0') {
        deck.push(card);
      }
    }
  }
}
```

```javascript
// Add the wild and wild draw four cards
for (let wild of wilds) {
  for (let i = 0; i < 4; i++) {
    deck.push({
      color: 'Wild',
      value: wild
    });
  }
}
  return deck;
}
let unoDeck = createUnoDeck();
// Shuffle the deck
unoDeck.sort(() => Math.random() - 0.5);
console.log(unoDeck);
```

This script creates a deck of UNO cards, with each card represented as an object with `color` and `value` properties. It then shuffles the deck and logs the shuffled deck to the console.

Judging by that response, I'd say it knows exactly what Uno cards are. I must admit to being impressed with what it gave me. It produced functional, well-documented code, and its typical explanation of what it generated.

It did not initially honor my prior request to wrap lines at 60 characters, though. I had to remind it.

Grocery shopping list

This one might not come up quite as often for demo use, but it's still an interesting exercise.

ChatGPT 4 doesn't always seem to understand whether it should take prior instructions into account. Perhaps my pivot to cards threw it off.

> Create an array of possible grocery items
>
> Sure, here's a simple array of possible grocery items:
>
> ```
> const groceryItems = [
>   'Apples', 'Bananas', 'Oranges', 'Strawberries',
>   'Grapes', 'Lettuce', 'Tomatoes', 'Cucumbers',
>   'Carrots', 'Bell Peppers', 'Onions', 'Garlic',
>   'Potatoes', 'Chicken', 'Beef', 'Pork', 'Salmon',
>   'Tilapia', 'Rice', 'Pasta', 'Bread', 'Eggs',
>   'Milk', 'Butter', 'Cheese', 'Yogurt', 'Ice Cream',
>   'Coffee', 'Tea', 'Juice', 'Water', 'Soda',
>   'Cereal', 'Oatmeal', 'Flour', 'Sugar', 'Salt',
>   'Pepper', 'Olive Oil', 'Canola Oil', 'Vinegar',
>   'Baking Powder', 'Baking Soda'
> ];
> ```
>
> This list includes a variety of fruits, vegetables, meats, grains, dairy products, beverages, and baking ingredients. It's not exhaustive, of course—there are many other items you could find in a grocery store!

It is literally what I asked for, but not exactly what I was expecting. When I tried this before on ChatGPT with GPT 3.5, I got a completely different list, and much closer to what I had expected. I'll show it here for comparison.

```
// Create an array of possible grocery items
const groceryItems = ['Apples', 'Bananas', 'Oranges', 'Lemons', 'Lettuce', 'Carrots', 'Potatoes', 'Onions', 'Tomatoes', 'Garlic', 'Ground Beef', 'Chicken Breasts', 'Eggs', 'Milk', 'Cheese', 'Bread', 'Pasta', 'Rice', 'Beans', 'Cereal', 'Yogurt'];

// Create an empty array to store the random grocery list
const randomList = [];

// Function to generate a random number of items
function randomNumberOfItems() {
  return Math.floor(Math.random() * groceryItems.length);
}

// Loop through the groceryItems array and push a random number of items to the randomList array
for (let i = 0; i < randomNumberOfItems(); i++) {
  randomList.push(groceryItems[Math.floor(Math.random() * groceryItems.length)]);
}

console.log(randomList);
```

In the GPT 3.5 version, it seemed to understand that I wasn't simply looking for a list of objects (what I actually asked for), but it inferred that I wanted to use that list as part of a larger application. This is the first time I have seen GPT 4 underperform GPT 3.5.

What do you think? Is it better or worse? GPT 4 did exactly what I asked it to do and did not embellish.

Stock market symbols

What I most appreciate about ChatGPT is that it usually understands context. It knows what I mean by "Stock Symbols." It gave me a very thorough code block. However, as with the grocery list, GPT 3.5 did a better job of understanding what I really wanted. Let me show you both.

GPT 3.5

Create a list of random stock symbols
// Create an array of possible stock symbols
const stockSymbols = ['AAPL', 'GOOGL', 'AMZN', 'FB', 'MSFT', 'BABA', 'TATAMOTORS', 'BA', 'INFY', 'WMT', 'GE', 'CVX', 'PG', 'XOM', 'CMCSA', 'C'];
// Create an empty array to store the random stock symbols
const randomStockSymbols = [];
// Function to generate a random number of stock symbols
function randomNumberOfSymbols() {
return Math.floor(Math.random() * stockSymbols.length);
}
// Loop through the stockSymbols array and push a random number of symbols to the randomStockSymbols array
for (let i = 0; i < randomNumberOfSymbols(); i++) {
randomStockSymbols.push(stockSymbols[Math.floor(Math.random() * stockSymbols.length)]);
}
console.log(randomStockSymbols);

GPT 4

As with the grocery list, GPT 4 took me literally. It wrote me code that would generate "random" stock symbols.

> Create a list of random stock symbols
>
> Here's an example of generating an array of random stock symbols in JavaScript. In this case, I will create 10 symbols made up of random uppercase letters:
>
> ```javascript
> function generateRandomStockSymbols(n) {
>   let symbols = [];
>   for (let i = 0; i < n; i++) {
>     let symbol = '';
>     for (let j = 0; j < 4; j++) {
>       symbol += String.fromCharCode(
>         Math.floor(Math.random() * 26) + 65
>       );
>     }
>     symbols.push(symbol);
>   }
>   return symbols;
> }
> let stockSymbols = generateRandomStockSymbols(10);
> console.log(stockSymbols);
> ```
>
> The `generateRandomStockSymbols` function generates `n` stock symbols. Each symbol is a string of 4 random uppercase letters. The `String.fromCharCode` function is used to convert a Unicode value into a character, and `Math.floor(Math.random() * 26) + 65` generates a random

> number between 65 and 90, the Unicode values for 'A' and 'Z', respectively.
>
> Please note that these are not real stock symbols, just random strings of letters. Real stock symbols have specific meanings and are assigned to companies by the stock exchange.

This is closer to what I got when I asked GitHub Copilot to do the same thing. It, too, simply gave me a random list of random characters.

When you are using ChatGPT for your own code and projects, switch between GPT 3.5 and 4 often to see which one gives you better results.

Random stock price stream

Can it also provide a random price stream from one of those symbols? Remember, ChatGPT is supposed to know about your context and remember your conversations. As before, GPT 4 and GPT 3.5 seem to diverge when asked to do similar tasks.

ChatGPT 4

> Generate an observable stream of prices for each stock, changing every 5 seconds
>
> To create an observable stream, we can use the RxJS library in JavaScript, which provides the Observable class among other reactive programming features. Here's how you could create an observable stream of prices for each stock that emits a new value every 5 seconds:
>
> ```
> const { Observable, interval } = require('rxjs');
> const { map } = require('rxjs/operators');
> function generateRandomStockSymbols(n) {
> ```

```
// Code to generate random stock symbols
// goes here...
}
function generatePriceStream(symbol) {
  return interval(5000).pipe(
    map(() => ({
      symbol: symbol,
      price: (Math.random() * 1000).toFixed(2)
    }))
  );
}
const stockSymbols = generateRandomStockSymbols(10);
const priceStreams = stockSymbols.map(
  symbol => generatePriceStream(symbol)
);
priceStreams.forEach(stream => {
  stream.subscribe(price => console.log(price));
});
```

This code creates an observable for each stock symbol that emits a new price every 5 seconds. The price is a random number between 0 and 1000.

The `interval` function creates an Observable that emits sequential numbers every specified interval of time—in this case, every 5000 milliseconds (5 seconds). The `map` operator is then used to transform these numbers into objects representing stock prices.

Finally, a subscription is created for each price stream, which

> logs the emitted prices to the console.
>
> Note: Please make sure to have RxJS installed in your project.
>
> Also, this code is an example and doesn't include any real-world stock market logic. The prices are purely random and do not represent any real-world value.

I like how it didn't repeat the code to generate the random stock symbols, but simply told me to call it. I suppose that's a win, as it didn't waste my time giving me something that it already had. That is not what it usually does, though. Most of the time, it'll happily recreate the last answer, only modifying it slightly.

ChatGPT 3.5

The code I got from GPT 3.5 was similar to what GPT 4 gave me, but far more useful for a demo app. As with past prompts, it insists on giving a complete answer to every question. Here is what it gave me in its entirety.

> Generate an observable stream of prices for each stock, changing every 5 seconds
>
> ```
> const { Observable } = rxjs;
> ```
>
> ```
> // Create an array of possible stock symbols
> ```
>
> ```
> const stockSymbols = ['AAPL', 'GOOGL', 'AMZN', 'FB', 'MSFT', 'BABA', 'TATAMOTORS', 'BA', 'INFY', 'WMT', 'GE', 'CVX', 'PG', 'XOM', 'CMCSA', 'C'];
> ```
>
> ```
> // Create an empty array to store the random stock symbols
> ```
>
> ```
> const randomStockSymbols = [];
> ```
>
> ```
> // Function to generate a random number of stock symbols
> ```
>
> ```
> function randomNumberOfSymbols() {
> ```

```
  return Math.floor(Math.random() * stockSymbols.length);
}
// Loop through the stockSymbols array and push a random number of symbols to the randomStockSymbols array
for (let i = 0; i < randomNumberOfSymbols(); i++) {

randomStockSymbols.push(stockSymbols[Math.floor(Math.random() * stockSymbols.length)]);
}
console.log(randomStockSymbols);
// Create an empty array to store the random stock prices
const randomStockPrices = [];
// Function to generate a random stock price
function randomStockPrice() {
  return (Math.random() * (300 - 50) + 50).toFixed(2);
}
// Loop through the randomStockSymbols array and push a random stock price to the randomStockPrices array
for (let i = 0; i < randomStockSymbols.length; i++) {
  const stock = {
    symbol: randomStockSymbols[i],
    price: randomStockPrice()
  };
  randomStockPrices.push(stock);
}
console.log(randomStockPrices);
```

```
// Create an observable stream for each stock symbol
const stockStreams = randomStockSymbols.map(symbol => {
  return Observable.create(observer => {
    setInterval(() => {
      observer.next({
        symbol,
        price: randomStockPrice()
      });
    }, 5000);
  });
});

// Subscribe to each stock stream and log the updated stock price
stockStreams.forEach(stream => {
  stream.subscribe(stock => {
    console.log(`${stock.symbol}: $${stock.price}`);
  });
});
```

This code generates an observable stream for each stock symbol in the **randomStockSymbols** array, using the **rxjs** library and the **Observable.create()** method. It uses the **setInterval()** function to emit a new stock object containing the symbol and a random price every 5 seconds. Then it subscribes to each stock stream and logs the updated stock price.

It's important to note that for this code to work, you should import **rxjs** library first.

Conclusion

Overall, I rate ChatGPT 4 a 7 or 8 out of 10 on the success scale. It ended up taking me more literally than I would have liked. Honestly, though, that may be a good thing. It really comes down to the prompt. It does a great job, considering what it's designed to do.

ChatGPT 3.5 seemed to understand what I wanted more than what I said, which is nice. Either one of them remembers past requests, so you can give instructions such as, "Do that again, using single quotes instead of double quotes." Or "Rewrite that function using built-in JavaScript array functions." One downside of ChatGPT that I did not show is that every time you ask it to rewrite or refactor an earlier answer, it slowly regenerates the entire block. After five or six of those, the time it takes to generate its answers feels longer and longer.

ChatGPT 3.5 is faster than 4, which was unexpected. I did discover later that ChatGPT Plus, the paid subscription version, generates code much faster. I guess that's what you get for $20/month (price as of May 2023).

AGILE PROJECT MANAGEMENT

Image by 14995841 from Pixabay

I'm going to make an admission here. I am not a fan of project management tasks. I don't like creating stories, grooming stories, doing project estimates, etc. I want to build working code and do it as fast as possible.

However, I do recognize the value of project management tasks. That's where AI comes into play. AI can help make the process a little simpler and more pleasant by automating certain aspects of the project management process. For example, AI-powered tools can assist with story grooming by creating comprehensive user acceptance criteria.

This gets these tasks off my plate as quickly as possible, so that I can get to the more interesting job of delivering software. In this chapter, I'll show you how I use ChatGPT for project planning.

Project Concept

I started by describing an application to ChatGPT. The application in question is the demo application from a few of my books and video courses.

> Act as my chief marketing officer. Our company makes mobile apps. We're about to create a brand new application. It will store and manage the student attendance for a single classroom. It will store the names and contact information for the class roster and the students' parents. It will provide a way to add, edit, and remove students, as well as the ability to mark the students absent or present for a given day. The app will run on both desktop web, iOS, and Android. It will also connect to the device's camera to add a photograph of each student.
>
> Write a marketing summary for it.

I gave that description to ChatGPT and asked it "to write a marketing summary for it." Here is its reply. Notice that it even made up a name for my new app!

> **Marketing Summary: ClassCheck – A Comprehensive Student Attendance Management App**
>
> ClassCheck is an innovative application that revolutionizes the way classroom attendance is managed. As we transition into an increasingly digital era, we believe it's time for schools

to have a modern, simple, and efficient solution to track and manage student attendance. ClassCheck is designed to empower educators, administrators, and parents alike, helping them stay organized and informed.

Harnessing the power of web and mobile technologies, ClassCheck is a versatile platform that runs on desktop web, iOS, and Android. It provides an intuitive and user-friendly interface that allows users to easily add, edit, and remove student profiles, mark attendance, and maintain an up-to-date class roster.

One of the standout features of ClassCheck is its ability to store contact information not only for students, but also their parents, fostering effective communication between the school and home. This feature ensures that parents are informed of their children's attendance patterns and can stay involved in their academic journey.

Furthermore, ClassCheck integrates seamlessly with your device's camera, enabling users to add photographs of each student. This visual aspect enhances the personalization of student profiles and aids in easy identification, particularly useful in larger classrooms.

At its core, ClassCheck is more than just an attendance app. It's a comprehensive tool designed to streamline the administrative tasks associated with managing a classroom. It's about keeping parents informed, helping teachers manage their time more efficiently, and ultimately, promoting student success.

ClassCheck - Modernize your classroom management. Stay organized, stay connected, and foster success with our all-in-one attendance management application.

It almost makes me want to go out and buy the app! ChatGPT 3.5 gave me a much less ambitious response, which I was happy with at the time.

> "Attendance Manager" is a multi-platform app that simplifies classroom attendance management. With its easy-to-use interface, you can quickly store and manage the names, contact information, and attendance records of students and their parents. The app features a photo capturing capability, which makes student identification quick and effortless. Whether you are on a desktop computer or a mobile device, Attendance Manager ensures that you have access to your class roster and attendance records anytime, anywhere. Experience the ease and convenience of attendance management with Attendance Manager!

How great is that!? Beginning with a dry application description, I got a decent description suitable for use as a starting point for a market brochure. More importantly for my purposes is that I can then build on that to help with the rest of the project plan.

Epics and User Stories

Next, I asked it to use that description to generate my epics and user stories for this admittedly simple application.

For simplicity, I'll show GPT 3.5 separately only if there is a noticeable difference.

> Given that description, create a few agile epics that will help direct the development of the application. I envision three different visual screens for the application. A home page, a roster page, and a student details page. Add those to the epics and stories.
>
> **Epic 1: Home Page Development**
>
> Story 1.1: As a user, I should be able to easily navigate to

different sections of the application from the home page.

Story 1.2: As a user, I want to see an overview of class attendance status on the home page, so that I can quickly understand if there are any unusual patterns or issues.

Story 1.3: As a user, I should have access to important notifications or updates on the home page, so that I can stay informed about critical information.

Epic 2: Roster Page Development

Story 2.1: As a user, I need to be able to view the complete class roster on a dedicated page, so that I can have a full overview of my class.

Story 2.2: As a user, I want to sort and filter the class roster based on different criteria (e.g., attendance, alphabetical order), so that I can easily find specific information.

Story 2.3: As a user, I should be able to click on a student's name to view their detailed profile, so that I can get more information about a particular student.

Epic 3: Student Details Page Development

Story 3.1: As a user, I need to see detailed information about a student (e.g., attendance record, contact details) on their profile page, so that I can understand their individual situation better.

Story 3.2: As a user, I should be able to edit a student's information or mark their attendance directly from their profile page, so that I can quickly update their records.

Story 3.3: As a user, I want to be able to add, change or remove a student's photograph on their profile page, so that their visual identification is kept up-to-date.

Epic 4: Cross-Platform Compatibility

Story 4.1: As a user, I want the application to function

> seamlessly across desktop, iOS, and Android platforms, so I can use it on my preferred device.
>
> Story 4.2: As a user, I expect the application's UI/UX to be intuitive and consistent across platforms, so I have a positive user experience.
>
> **Epic 5: Parent-Teacher Communication Enhancement**
>
> Story 5.1: As a user, I should be able to contact parents directly from the application (via email or phone), so that I can quickly communicate important information.
>
> Story 5.2: As a user, I want to send automated attendance notifications to parents, so they can stay updated about their child's attendance.

This is more than I would have come up with on my own, and the user stories are easily good enough to get started planning the project. Keep in mind that this took a only a few seconds.

ChatGPT 3.5 gave me enough of a different answer that it's worth showing here. It did the same thing, but it recognized that the "user" would be a "teacher." Subtle, but it might be important. I will only show the first one, though.

> Student Information Management:
>
> Epic: Manage Student Information
>
> As a teacher, I want to be able to add, edit, and remove students and their parents' contact information in the system.
>
> As a teacher, I want to be able to view a class roster and search for specific students.
>
> Story: Create Student Details Page
>
> As a teacher, I want to navigate to the student details page from

> the roster page to add, edit, or remove student information.
>
> As a teacher, I want to view a student's photo, name, and contact information on the student details page.

I think the GPT 4 answer is subjectively better, but GPT 3.5 understood my context a little more accurately. Again, try them both and see which one suits your application.

User Acceptance Criteria

Next, let's see what happened when I asked for some user acceptance criteria for these stories. I won't show them all here, just enough to give you an idea of what it does.

> Generate some user acceptance criteria for the stories in epic 1 using the "given, when, then" syntax
>
> Story 1.1: As a user, I should be able to easily navigate to different sections of the application from the home page.
>
> *Acceptance Criteria:*
>
> Given that I am on the home page,
>
> When I look at the navigation menu,
>
> Then I should see options to go to the "Roster Page" and "Student Details Page".
>
> ...

I cut it off intentionally because I didn't care for the format. Rather than trying to edit it, I simply asked ChatGPT to change the format and regenerate its output.

> Regenerate that AC without any blank lines between sections and keeping the given/then/when on the same line. There is no

reason to break it up like that. Also, don't bother with bold and italic. It doesn't paste into Word very well.

Story 1.1: As a user, I should be able to easily navigate to different sections of the application from the home page.

- Acceptance Criteria 1: Given that I am on the home page, when I look at the navigation menu, then I should see options to go to the "Roster Page" and "Student Details Page".

- Acceptance Criteria 2: Given that I am on the home page, when I select the "Roster Page" from the navigation menu, then I should be directed to the Roster Page.

- Acceptance Criteria 3: Given that I am on the home page, when I select the "Student Details Page" from the navigation menu, then I should be directed to the Student Details Page.

Story 1.2: As a user, I want to see an overview of class attendance status on the home page, so that I can quickly understand if there are any unusual patterns or issues.

- Acceptance Criteria 1: Given that I am on the home page, when I look at the overview section, then I should see a summary of the class attendance status.

- Acceptance Criteria 2: Given the class attendance status summary, when I observe the status, then I should be able to identify any unusual attendance patterns or issues.

Story 1.3: As a user, I should have access to important notifications or updates on the home page, so that I can stay informed about critical information.

- Acceptance Criteria 1: Given that I am on the home page, when I look at the notifications section, then I should see any new updates or important notifications.

- Acceptance Criteria 2: Given that there are new notifications, when I view them, then I should understand the critical information that affects the class or individual students.

It still insisted on using asterisks to bold the stories. But, as you can see, the format itself is easier to read.

GPT 3.5, as I've started to expect, gave me completely different acceptance criteria. It's simpler, but acceptable. However, if I am trying to use it because I don't want to write them, the more detailed output from GPT 4 is better.

> Generate some user acceptance criteria for the stories in epic 1 using the "given, when, then" syntax
>
> Manage Student Information - Create Student Details Page
>
> Given that I am a teacher using the application, when I navigate to the student details page from the roster page, then I should see an interface to add, edit, or remove student information.
>
> Acceptance Criteria:
>
> - The student details page is accessible from the roster page.
> - The interface displays the student's photo.
> - The interface includes fields for the student's name, contact information, and photo.
> - The interface allows the teacher to add a new student, edit existing student information, and remove a student.
> - The changes made in the interface are saved in the system.
>
> Manage Student Information - View Class Roster
>
> Given that I am a teacher using the application, when I view the class roster, then I should see a list of all students in the class and their contact information.

Acceptance Criteria:

- The class roster is accessible from the home page.
- The roster displays the student's photo, name, and contact information.
- The roster allows the teacher to search for a specific student.
- The roster is sorted alphabetically by student name.
- Manage Student Information - Search for Specific Students

Given that I am a teacher using the application, when I search for a specific student on the class roster, then I should see the matching students and their contact information.

Acceptance Criteria:

- The teacher can initiate a search on the class roster page.
- The search matches the student name, photo, and contact information with the search query.
- The search results are displayed in a list format.
- The search results are sorted alphabetically by student name.

The important thing to note is that ChatGPT took care of one of the most tedious tasks in software development, at least from where I'm sitting. Is it perfect? Not at all. There are features and acceptance criteria I never asked for. I didn't say anything about a search or attendance pattern features, but ChatGPT added them to my application. That doesn't mean I have to add those features.

There are a couple of ways to look at this. One is that it just suggested features I hadn't considered, but maybe should. The other is that I can simply ignore it or ask ChatGPT to regenerate the UAC without the extra features. Either way is a win for me.

GPT 3.5 also didn't write each of the acceptance criteria using "Given/when/then," but otherwise I'm happy with what it gave me.

By the way, I did ask it to generate UAC without using the term "user acceptance criteria." It tried to create "user access control" instead, which was a very different result.

Estimations

If there is a task most developers dislike more than generating stories and acceptance criteria, it would have to be estimations. Fortunately, I was able to get ChatGPT to manage that for me as well, at least partially, using T-Shirt sizing.

T-Shirt Sizing

In case you aren't familiar with the concept, T-Shirt sizing is a method of estimation that assigns relative sizes to tasks or features based on their perceived level of difficulty. The sizing is usually done using a set of labels, such as XS (extra small), S (small), M (medium), L (large), XL (extra-large), and so on, to indicate the relative size of each task.

The exact labels and their meanings may vary between organizations, but the goal is to provide a rough, relative estimate that can be used for planning and prioritization purposes. The method is named after the idea of T-shirts being different sizes, with a small T-shirt being easier to handle than a large one.

With that understanding, I asked ChatGPT:

> Given the relative difficulties of those tasks and their UAC, generate a rough relative estimate for each using T-shirt sizing.
>
> Using T-shirt sizing, the rough estimates for the tasks in Epic 1 could be as follows:
>
> Story 1.1: As a user, I should be able to easily navigate to different sections of the application from the home page.
>
> - Size: Medium. Navigation is a basic requirement for most applications and usually doesn't involve complex functionalities, but it does require careful UX design and testing to ensure it works intuitively.
>
> Story 1.2: As a user, I want to see an overview of class attendance status on the home page, so that I can quickly understand if there are any unusual patterns or issues.
>
> - Size: Large. This requirement involves the real-time computation and visualization of attendance data, which could be complex depending on the exact nature of the overview (e.g., graphs, tables, etc.).
>
> Story 1.3: As a user, I should have access to important notifications or updates on the home page, so that I can stay informed about critical information.
>
> - Size: Medium. While creating a notifications system may not be overly complex, it requires careful planning to ensure that it delivers the right information at the right time and in a user-friendly manner..

What impressed me about the response is that it attempted to justify its estimates. With this as a starting point, I would feel a lot more comfortable creating some estimates for management. If nothing else, it gives the team a place to begin a longer discussion.

Fibonacci Estimates

While T-Shirt Sizing is often enough for the development team, management typically wants something a little more concrete. My team uses Fibonacci values.

The idea behind using Fibonacci numbers is that each number represents a rough estimate of the amount of effort required to complete a task or feature, and the gap between each number becomes progressively larger as the estimate becomes larger. This helps to avoid the use of overly precise estimates, which can be difficult to achieve and lead to unachievable expectations.

This method allows for the estimation of tasks with a high degree of uncertainty, where the exact effort required is not known. By using a set of standardized values, teams can make rough estimates that are consistent and easily understood across the organization.

I asked ChatGPT to rewrite its T-Shirt estimates as Fibonacci instead. It generated almost the same text as before, but with different values, which is exactly what I expected.

> Rewrite those T-Shirt estimates as Fibonacci values instead
>
> Using the Fibonacci sequence for rough estimates, the equivalent points for the tasks in Epic 1 could be:
>
> Story 1.1: As a user, I should be able to easily navigate to different sections of the application from the home page.
>
> - Points: 3. Navigation is a basic requirement for most applications and usually doesn't involve complex

functionalities, but it does require careful UX design and testing to ensure it works intuitively.

Story 1.2: As a user, I want to see an overview of class attendance status on the home page, so that I can quickly understand if there are any unusual patterns or issues.

- Points: 5. This requirement involves the real-time computation and visualization of attendance data, which could be complex depending on the exact nature of the overview (e.g., graphs, tables, etc.).

Story 1.3: As a user, I should have access to important notifications or updates on the home page, so that I can stay informed about critical information.

- Points: 3. While creating a notifications system may not be overly complex, it requires careful planning to ensure that it delivers the right information at the right time and in a user-friendly manner.

Summary

ChatGPT can be used to write concise and clear marketing summaries, create agile epics and user stories, generate user acceptance criteria, and provide rough estimates. It can help streamline the process by providing fast and accurate responses. The use of ChatGPT in in this way can help you achieve greater efficiency and consistency, especially if (like me) you don't particularly care for these tasks.

I've been using this strategy personally and as a result, I'm enjoying the process more than ever before. I find staring at a blank screen to be hard, but I don't mind rephrasing and refining the output ChatGPT gives me for these tasks.

LET'S BUILD AN APP!

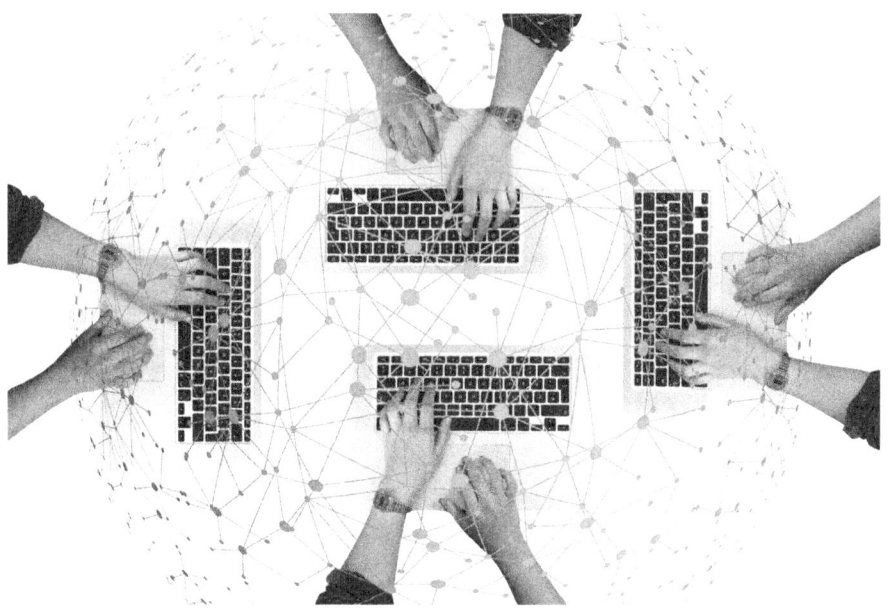

Image by Gerd Altmann from Pixabay

In the previous chapters, I included very verbose output from ChatGPT to show how well or poorly it did with the given prompts.

For this chapter, I'm going to ask ChatGPT, as my pair programming companion, to build a modest application with as little input from me as possible.

My technology stack will be a web application with HTML, Angular, and the Ionic Framework. Those choices are tangential to the point of using AI as my companion. Those are what I use every day, so I will quickly know whether or not the code generated by the AI is accurate.

If you aren't familiar with it, Ionic is a popular web framework for building applications of all types, but it has traditionally been used to create hybrid mobile applications. That is, mobile apps written with web technologies.

It won't be a complicated app, just enough to demonstrate how I use the tools.

Hopefully you will follow along. If you do, let me know how it goes.

Is This a Good Idea?

Honestly, I almost didn't include this chapter at all. I wasn't sure whether ChatGPT made sense for this type of work. My hesitation about using ChatGPT for this chapter is twofold:

1. There is a lot of back-and-forth when coding. If you're in and out of the editor, back to ChatGPT, etc. It gets tiresome quickly. I thought a tool such as GitHub Copilot would be better, since you never leave your editor.

2. ChatGPT doesn't know about anything past September 2021. What versions of Angular and Ionic were current then? I decided to ask ChatGPT to find out.

> What is the newest version of Angular and Ionic Framework you know of?
>
> I'm sorry for any confusion, but as an AI model, my training data only includes information up to September 2021, and I can't access real-time information or updates. As of my last update, the latest stable version of Angular was Angular 12,

> released in May 2021, and Ionic was at version 5, released in February 2020.
>
> For the most current information, I recommend checking the official websites or relevant developer communities for Angular and Ionic.

Angular 12 is now out of support, with 16 released in May 2023. Likewise, Ionic 7 was just released. That said, I know versions 16 and 5 respectively are current enough that the code it generates *should be* fine, so I decided to make the most comprehensive prompt I could think of and see what it would give me. Here it is in its entirety.

> Using Angular and the Ionic Framework, create a complete web application that uses a split-pane layout with a side menu and a default Home page. It should have an Angular service to load blog posts from a remote sample API. Those blog posts should be displayed on a page called Posts. The Posts page should be responsive, displaying the blog post titles and body in an <ion-card>. When working with Observables, prefer the async pipe over subscribing and unsubscribing. Make sure you provide the Ionic CLI commands to create the application and any additional items needed to create the application. Each page should have a header bar, including menu and back buttons where appropriate. Provide the code and just explanation for me to build it. In your explanations, don't add any blank lines between paragraphs. Ensure that all code wraps at 60 characters.
>
> Sure, I will guide you through the creation of this app. I'll be using Angular 12 and Ionic 5 for this guide, as those are the latest versions at my knowledge cutoff in September 2021. You may need to adjust the commands if you're using later versions.

1. Install Ionic CLI: If you haven't already installed the Ionic CLI, do it with this command:

```
npm install -g @ionic/cli
```

2. Start a new Ionic project:

```
ionic start myApp sidemenu --type=angular
```

This command creates a new Ionic app named `myApp` with a side menu layout.

3. Generate the Posts page:

```
ionic generate page Posts
```

4. Generate a service to fetch blog posts:

```
ionic generate service services/posts
```

5. Modify the Posts service (`src/app/services/posts.service.ts`):

```
import { Injectable } from '@angular/core';
import { HttpClient } from '@angular/common/http';
import { Observable } from 'rxjs';
import { Post } from '../models/post.model';

@Injectable({
  providedIn: 'root'
})
export class PostsService {
    private postsUrl = 'https://jsonplaceholder.typicode.com/posts';
    constructor(private http: HttpClient) { }
    getPosts(): Observable<Post[]> {
      return this.http.get<Post[]>(this.postsUrl);
```

}

}

This service uses Angular's `HttpClient` to fetch blog posts from a remote API. You need to import `HttpClientModule` in your `app.module.ts` file.

6. Create a Post model (`src/app/models/post.model.ts`):

```
export class Post {
  userId: number;
  id: number;
  title: string;
  body: string;
}
```

7. Modify the Posts page (`src/app/posts/posts.page.ts`):

```
import { Component, OnInit } from '@angular/core';
import { Observable } from 'rxjs';
import { PostsService } from '../services/posts.service';
import { Post } from '../models/post.model';
@Component({
  selector: 'app-posts',
  templateUrl: './posts.page.html',
  styleUrls: ['./posts.page.scss'],
})
export class PostsPage implements OnInit {
  posts$: Observable<Post[]>;
  constructor(private postsService: PostsService) { }
  ngOnInit() {
```

```
    this.posts$ = this.postsService.getPosts();
  }
}
```

Here, we're injecting the `PostsService` and initializing the `posts$` observable in the `ngOnInit` lifecycle hook.

8. Modify the Posts page template (`src/app/posts/posts.page.html`):

```
<ion-header>
  <ion-toolbar>
    <ion-buttons slot="start">
      <ion-menu-button></ion-menu-button>
    </ion-buttons>
    <ion-title>Posts</ion-title>
  </ion-toolbar>
</ion-header>
<ion-content>
  <ion-card *ngFor="let post of posts$ | async">
    <ion-card-header>
      <ion-card-title>{{ post.title }}</ion-card-title>
    </ion-card-header>
    <ion-card-content>
      {{ post.body }}
    </ion-card-content>
  </ion-card>
</ion-content>
```

This page displays a list of blog posts using `<ion-card>`. Each card displays the blog post title and body.

9. Add the Posts page to the side menu by modifying `app.component.ts` (`src/app/app.component.ts`) and app.component.html (`src/app/app.component.html`):

In `app.component.ts`, add the Posts page to the `appPages` array:

```
public appPages = [
  { title: 'Home', url: '/home', icon: 'home' },
  { title: 'Posts', url: '/posts', icon: 'list' }
];
```

In `app.component.html`, modify the `ion-menu-toggle` section:

```
<ion-menu-toggle auto-hide="false" *ngFor="let p of appPages">
  <ion-item [routerDirection]="'root'" [routerLink]="p.url">
    <ion-icon slot="start" [name]="p.icon"></ion-icon>
    <ion-label>
      {{ p.title }}
    </ion-label>
  </ion-item>
</ion-menu-toggle>
```

10. Add routing for the Posts page in `app-routing.module.ts` (`src/app/app-routing.module.ts`):

```
const routes: Routes = [
  {
    path: '',
    redirectTo: 'home',
```

```
    pathMatch: 'full'
  },
  {
    path: 'home',
      loadChildren: () => import('./home/home.module').then(m => m.HomePageModule)
  },
  {
    path: 'posts',
      loadChildren: () => import('./posts/posts.module').then(m => m.PostsPageModule)
  }
];
```

11. Run the app:

```
ionic serve
```

This command will start a local development server for your app. Open your web browser and navigate to `http://localhost:8100` to see your app.

The application should now display a side menu with Home and Posts. The Posts page will display a list of blog posts fetched from the remote API, and it should be responsive, adjusting its layout according to the screen size. The use of the async pipe with the `posts$` observable ensures that Angular will automatically manage subscriptions, eliminating the need for manual subscribe and unsubscribe calls.

That is pretty thorough, though it forgot to give me a back button on my Posts page. It also didn't wrap its code to 60 characters. If I were just starting to write an app, though, I can think of far worse ways to begin.

I didn't enter all this in, but it looks like it will work.

When I first tried this a few months ago with GPT 3.5, the best I could say about its response was that it gave me a pretty good start.

This is where I think I prefer tools like GitHub Copilot. Copilot often needs some coaxing, but it mostly gets the code right, and its knowledge is more up to date. You can easily delete a line or a function, type a new comment, and quickly get the code you need.

With ChatGPT, you can ask it to refine its response, but it will usually generate everything again. Not only that, but I've seen it generate completely different code on subsequent passes, changing more than you ask it to.

As an Ionic Developer Expert (I am – look it up), I'm not entirely convinced ChatGPT would have saved me much time here. I still like it for writing simple functions and algorithms.

Though it's gotten better, I'm not sure it's suited for writing complete apps (yet?). With the improvements I've seen just over the past few months, maybe it will be very soon.

UNIT TESTING

Image by Gerd Altmann from Pixabay

As developers, we know the importance of unit testing in ensuring the quality and reliability of our software. Yet, we also know the struggles that come with creating effective unit tests - the time and effort required, the complexity of the testing process, and the challenge of ensuring comprehensive coverage. Personally, I have often found myself skipping unit tests in the interest of saving time, only to regret it later when bugs and errors inevitably arise.

In this chapter, we will explore how ChatGPT can help ease the pain of creating effective unit tests, by generating test cases for a simple Angular service. Through this process, we will see how these tools can help enhance the unit testing process.

The Service

The service itself is simple enough. I wanted to

build a means of setting and retrieving two different unique IDs my app can use when making service calls. The first is a "conversation ID" that will be set as an HTTP header for all network calls for a specific user for a given session. It will not change until the application user manually refreshes the screen, closes the browser, or logs out and back in.

The second is a "correlation ID." This will also get sent with each HTTP call, but it changes with every request. I won't show the network calls, just the service to generate the IDs.

The Service API

There are three primary requirements the service implements.

1. It will give me the same conversation ID whenever I ask, unless one does not exist. In that case, it needs to give me a new one and return it.
2. It will give me a fresh correlation ID every time I request one. I should never get the same ID twice.
3. It will provide a way for me to force a fresh conversation ID.

The implementation will use UUIDs for both the conversationId and the correlationId. In case you aren't aware of the term UUID, I asked ChatGPT to define it:

> What is a UUID?
>
> UUID stands for Universally Unique Identifier. This is a 128-bit number used to uniquely identify information in computer

systems. The term globally unique identifier (GUID) is also used, typically in software created by Microsoft.

When generated according to the standard methods, UUIDs are, for practical purposes, unique. Their uniqueness does not depend on a central registration authority or coordination between the parties generating them, unlike most other numbering schemes.

A typical UUID looks like this:

`550e8400-e29b-41d4-a716-446655440000`

It's broken down into five parts:

1. A 32-bit time_low

2. A 16-bit time_mid

3. A 16-bit time_hi_and_version

4. An 8-bit clock_seq_hi_and_reserved

5. An 8-bit clock_seq_low

6. A 48-bit node

The string representation of a UUID consists of 32 alphanumeric characters separated by hyphens.

UUIDs are widely used in software construction as database keys, component identifiers, or just about anywhere else a truly unique identifier is required. UUIDs are also used to assign unique reference numbers to objects that may be distributed across a network, or to identify specific power supplies to help prevent hardware conflict.

That is far more complete than I got from GPT 3.5:

A UUID, or Universally Unique Identifier, is a type of identifier that is used to uniquely identify information in a distributed system. A UUID is a 128-bit number represented as a sequence of hexadecimal digits, typically displayed in groups separated by hyphens. UUIDs are designed to be unique across both space and time, meaning that they should never collide or be duplicated, even if generated by different systems at different times. UUIDs are commonly used in a variety of contexts, including as keys in databases, as identifiers for files or objects in storage systems, and as session IDs in web applications. The use of UUIDs helps to ensure that there is no ambiguity or conflict when multiple systems need to refer to the same entity, and also helps to provide an additional layer of security by making it more difficult to guess or manipulate identifiers.

In short, UUIDs are perfect identifiers to use for my purposes in identifying and correlating HTTP calls across various systems.

The code itself small and straightforward. I will reproduce the entirety of the service here for reference.

```
import { Injectable } from '@angular/core';
import { v4 as uuidv4 } from 'uuid';
@Injectable({
  providedIn: 'root'
})
export class CorrelationService {
  conversationId: string = '';
  resetConversationId() {
    this.conversationId = uuidv4();
    return this.conversationId;
  }
  getConversationId() {
```

```
  return this.conversationId || this.resetConversationId();
}
getCorrelationId() {
  return uuidv4();
}
}
```

There are three functions:

- **resetConversationId**: creates a brand new UUID and assigns it to the internal **coversationId** variable and returns that new value.
- **getConversationId**: returns the internal **conversationId** if it has a value, or calls resetConversationID and returns its result.
- **getCorrelationId**: simply returns a new UUID every time it's called.

As I said, it is a very simple service.

The Testing Framework

I want to start by reviewing the test code that is automatically generated by the Angular CLI. I do not mean for this to be a comprehensive introduction to testing, but I will explain the basics. It should be enough for you to follow along in your own tests.

By default, when you use the Angular CLI to create a service, it will also create a default test file. In my case, it created this for me.

```
import { TestBed } from '@angular/core/testing';
import { CorrelationService } from './correlation.service';
```

```
describe('CorrelationService', () => {
  let service: CorrelationService;
  beforeEach(() => {
    TestBed.configureTestingModule({});
    service = TestBed.inject(CorrelationService);
  });
  it('should be created', () => {
    expect(service).toBeTruthy();
  });
});
```

The first `import` line brings in the Angular testing class called `TestBed`. This class contains most of the basic testing framework.

The second pulls in the service to be tested, also known as the "System Under Test," or SUT. This is assigned to the variable `service`.

describe

```
describe('CorrelationService', () => {
```

With most JavaScript testing frameworks, tests are organized into one or more `describe` functions. These functions encapsulate related tests and isolate the inner tests from other, unrelated tests. They can be nested, as you will see shortly.

The `describe` function is called with two parameters.

1. The test label. In this case, the name of the service to be tested.

2. The function that contains the tests themselves. Here it is an arrow function. It contains a single variable representing the service, but nothing is assigned to it yet.

beforeEach

```
beforeEach(() => {
  TestBed.configureTestingModule({});
  service = TestBed.inject(CorrelationService);
});
```

Directly inside this function is another function call, `beforeEach`, which itself contains another arrow function. This function is called by the testing framework before every unit test is executed.

Inside this function is a call to `TestBed.configureTestingModule({})`, and you can see that it is being passed an empty object as its only argument. This object contains the test module's options. It can accept just about every option a normal Angular module can. Most tests use this to configure Angular's dependency injection system to inject test doubles required by the SUT. My service has no dependencies, so there is nothing to configure.

Other Functions

Not shown are some other functions that can contain setup/tear-down instructions:

- `beforeAll`: called once before any tests inside the `describe` are run. This is typically used to set up the state required by all tests, but which won't change from test to test.

- **afterEach**: called after each unit test function in the `describe`. This is used to tear down or reset the state to undo any side effects that a test might have created.
- **afterAll**: called once after all tests in the `describe` have been run. Again, this is used to reset the global state so that effects from your `describe` function don't bleed into others.

it

```
it('should be created', () => {
  expect(service).toBeTruthy();
});
```

This function defines a single unit test. You can create as many `it` functions as you want inside your `describe`. The generated test comes with a single `it` function. Its signature matches that of `describe`, in that it takes a label and a function defining the test.

When combined with its enclosing describe, the `it` functions should read like this:

[describe Label] [it Label]: Pass/Fail

Thus, when you read the one pre-generated test, it should look like this:

CorrelationService should be created: Pass

Consider this phrasing when you create your own tests.

There is a lot more to Angular testing than this, but I

wanted to make sure I explained what you would be seeing before I started.

The Tests

With that explanation out of the way, let's look at the tests ChatGPT generated for me. As we have seen throughout the book, the trick to getting ChatGPT to give you decent code is to provide it with the right prompt. For this prompt, it's best to give it the complete service implementation and ask it to write tests using Jasmine (or Jest if you prefer).

ChatGPT Responded with a complete test suite, as requested.

> Given the following Angular service, write a complete suite of unit tests using Jasmine. <I pasted the entire class code here>
>
> Sure, here's an example of how you might write a suite of unit tests using Jasmine for this service. The tests will check whether the `resetConversationId`, `getConversationId`, and `getCorrelationId` methods function as expected.

```
import { TestBed } from '@angular/core/testing';
import { CorrelationService } from './correlation.service';
import { v4 as uuidv4 } from 'uuid';
describe('CorrelationService', () => {
  let service: CorrelationService;
  beforeEach(() => {
    TestBed.configureTestingModule({});
    service = TestBed.inject(CorrelationService);
  });
  it('should be created', () => {
```

```
    expect(service).toBeTruthy();
  });
  describe('resetConversationId', () => {
    it('should reset the conversation ID', () => {
      spyOn(uuidv4, 'mock').and.returnValue('test-uuid');
      const id = service.resetConversationId();
      expect(id).toBe('test-uuid');
      expect(service.getConversationId()).toBe('test-uuid');
    });
  });
  describe('getConversationId', () => {
    it('should return the existing conversation ID if it exists', () => {
      service.conversationId = 'existing-uuid';
      const id = service.getConversationId();
      expect(id).toBe('existing-uuid');
    });
      it('should generate a new conversation ID if one does not exist', () => {
      spyOn(uuidv4, 'mock').and.returnValue('new-uuid');
      const id = service.getConversationId();
      expect(id).toBe('new-uuid');
    });
  });
  describe('getCorrelationId', () => {
    it('should generate a new correlation ID', () => {
```

```
    spyOn(uuidv4, 'mock').and.returnValue('correlation-uuid');
    const id = service.getCorrelationId();
    expect(id).toBe('correlation-uuid');
  });
 });
});
```

Please note that you will need to configure Jest to mock `uuidv4` in order for the tests to run as expected. You would typically do this in a setup file or directly in the test file.

The tests above cover the following scenarios:

- Whether the service is created correctly

- If `resetConversationId` resets the conversation ID as expected

- If `getConversationId` returns an existing ID if it exists, and generates a new one if it doesn't

- If `getCorrelationId` generates a new correlation ID as expected

Please replace `'mock'` with appropriate mocking method for your `uuidv4` package. Also, these tests assume that each ID generated is unique and cannot be predicted, so it focuses on the behavior of the methods rather than the specific values they return.

Interestingly, these tests won't work as-is. While they might look reasonable at first glance, ChatGPT got confused and told me I need to use Jest to mock the uuidv4 library. I asked it for Jasmine tests. GPT 3.5 actually gave me better results (which I won't reproduce), but even those tests didn't compile or run.

What's the takeaway here? As with the last chapter, ChatGPT will flood you with code that you either have to proofread carefully or accept at face value. Neither of these is an ideal situation.

Testing HTTP Calls

Testing a service is one thing. It's fairly simple and the pattern is straightforward once you've done it a few times. The real value we get from AI is in writing tests for things that aren't necessarily simple and straightforward, like testing HTTP calls.

This is something I know how to do conceptually but can never get the syntax right the first time. For example, I know I must import and use Angular's `HttpClientTestingModule`. There is a certain order that things have to be called and setup that has to be done. And every time, it's an exercise of trial and error until I get it right.

No longer.

I asked ChatGPT to help me write a test for a fictitious weather service. The service itself that I defined looks like this.

```
export class WeatherService {
  http: HttpClient = inject(HttpClient);
  getWeather(zipcode: string) {
    return this.http.get(`weather.com/api/forecast/${zipcode}`);
  }
}
```

ChatGPT gave me a pretty good test suite for this one.

> Consider the following code and write unit tests for my fictitious weather service. <I pasted the code from above>
>
> For testing this service, you would use the HttpClientTestingModule and HttpTestingController provided by Angular to create a mock version of HttpClient for testing. This allows you to control the requests made by the service and provide your own responses.
>
> Here's an example of how you could write the tests:

```typescript
import { HttpClientTestingModule, HttpTestingController } from '@angular/common/http/testing';
import { TestBed } from '@angular/core/testing';
import { HttpClient } from '@angular/common/http';
import { WeatherService } from './weather.service';

describe('WeatherService', () => {
  let service: WeatherService;
  let httpMock: HttpTestingController;

  beforeEach(() => {
    TestBed.configureTestingModule({
      imports: [HttpClientTestingModule],
      providers: [WeatherService]
    });

    service = TestBed.inject(WeatherService);
    httpMock = TestBed.inject(HttpTestingController);
  });

  afterEach(() => {
```

```
    httpMock.verify(); // Ensure that there are no outstanding requests
  });
  it('should be created', () => {
    expect(service).toBeTruthy();
  });
  describe('#getWeather', () => {
    it('should return the forecast for a given zip code', () => {
      const dummyForecast = {
        temperature: 20,
        conditions: 'Sunny'
      };
      service.getWeather('90210').subscribe(forecast => {
        expect(forecast).toEqual(dummyForecast);
      });
      const req = httpMock.expectOne('weather.com/api/forecast/90210');
      expect(req.request.method).toBe('GET');
      req.flush(dummyForecast);
    });
  });
});
```

In the above code:

- We create a TestBed that imports HttpClientTestingModule and provides WeatherService.

- Before each test, we get instances of WeatherService and

> HttpTestingController.
>
> - After each test, we call verify on the HttpTestingController to make sure that there are no outstanding requests.
>
> - In the test for getWeather, we subscribe to the method and set our expectations for what should happen when the request is made.
>
> - We use expectOne on the HttpTestingController to specify what URL we expect a request to be made to.
>
> - We check that the request made is a GET request.
>
> - Finally, we use flush on the request to return our dummyForecast as the response.;

It only handled the "happy path," but it gave me the structure I was looking for. As I implied, testing Angular's `HttpClient` is finicky, and I typically get it wrong the first time. Not only did ChatGPT get this one right, it explained its steps very well.

This is important for me because for some reason, I can never seem to remember to include the verification in `afterEach`, which assures that the service only made the expected HTTP calls, no more or less. Nor do I tend to remember the right order to create the mock's `expectOne` and `flush` functions.

Having ChatGPT build this test suite for me saves a lot of time. Once I have the structure in place, I can fill in the gaps (or perhaps get Copilot to do it for me).

This test passed the first time, by the way.

Far From Perfect

It's not all wine and roses, to be sure. We have already seen that ChatGPT doesn't know anything past mid-2021 or so. Other AI tools, such as Copilot, are better in this regard, as they are trained on more recent code, plus they can see your code.

I tried to get ChatGPT to help me write a unit test for an Angular `HttpInterceptor`, to use with the `CorrelationService` from the beginning of the chapter. I use an interceptor to add the `correlationId` and `coversationId` values as HTTP headers on every outgoing HTTP call.

ChatGPT knew about the class based `HttpInterceptor`, but nothing about the new functional `HttpInterceptorFn`, which was just introduced in Angular 15. It even insisted that no such thing exists.

Undoubtedly things will get better. For now, consider this one more piece of evidence that as good as the AI gets, we software developers still need to understand our craft. We can use these tools to help us, but we always need to be aware of their limitations.

OTHER CONSIDERATIONS

Image by Vicki Hamilton from Pixabay

When writing a book like this, it's hard to know when to stop. I see things on Twitter, people posting about all the cool stuff they're doing with AI. Naturally, I want to try them myself and add them to book. Ultimately, though, such an attitude becomes self-defeating. There are deadlines to meet and other projects the require my attention. I'm sure this isn't the last I'll write about this topic. I already have more ideas going through my head than is probably healthy. I doubt I'll ever get to all of them. However, there are a few interesting uses for AI that don't fit so neatly into any of the prior chapters. I want to take a few moments to touch on them here.

Understanding New Code

Throughout this book, I have been using AI to help with programming tasks. Another possibility is to use it the other way. ChatGPT is especially good at this. Consider the scenario where you have been given some legacy code and you aren't sure what it does (or exactly how). You can paste the code into ChatGPT and ask it for an explanation.

For example, I have some old Ionic/Angular/Firebase code in a project I haven't touched in a while. So, I asked ChatGPT what it does.

```
updateNames() {
  this.db
    .list('/hymns')
    .snapshotChanges()
    .pipe(
      first(),
      switchMap((list) => list)
    )
    .subscribe((hymn) => {
      hymn.payload.child('/arrangements').forEach((arrangement) => {
        const userNameNode = arrangement.child('/user/name');
        const names = userNameNode.val().split(' ');
        const maskedName = `${names[0]} ${names[names.length - 1][0]}.`;
        userNameNode.ref.set(maskedName);
```

```
      console.log(maskedName);
    });
    console.log('Done');
  });
}
```

What does that code do?

This JavaScript code appears to be using the Firebase Realtime Database, a cloud-hosted NoSQL database, and the RxJS library, which provides utilities for handling asynchronous operations and event-based programs. It's part of a function called `updateNames` which masks the names of users in a list of hymn arrangements. Let's break down what it's doing:

1. `this.db.list('/hymns').snapshotChanges()`: This line is getting a list of 'hymns' from a Firebase database and listening for changes on this list. The `snapshotChanges()` method provides information about both the data and its metadata, like the order or the URL of the data.

2. `.pipe(first(), switchMap((list) => list))`: Using the `pipe` function, it applies the `first()` operator to get the first item emitted by the source Observable (in this case, the list of hymns). Then, it applies the `switchMap` operator to map the items emitted by the source Observable (the list) to inner Observables.

3. `.subscribe((hymn) => { ... })`: This is where it subscribes to the Observable, meaning it will now execute code whenever the Observable emits an item (a hymn in this case).

4. Inside the `subscribe` function:

    - `hymn.payload.child('/arrangements').forEach((arrangement) => { ... })`: It's looping through each 'arrangement' child of the current 'hymn'.

- `const userNameNode = arrangement.child('/user/name');`: It's getting the 'name' child of the 'user' child of the current 'arrangement'.

- `const names = userNameNode.val().split(' ');`: It's splitting the user's name into parts by spaces.

- `const maskedName = `${names[0]} ${names[names.length - 1][0]}.`;`: It's creating a 'masked' version of the user's name, which includes the first name and the initial of the last name.

- `userNameNode.ref.set(maskedName);`: It's updating the user's name in the database to the masked version.

- `console.log(maskedName);`: It's logging the masked name to the console.

5. `console.log('Done');`: Once it has looped through all the arrangements of the hymn, it logs 'Done' to the console.

So, in summary, this code is listening for changes to a list of hymn arrangements in a Firebase database, and whenever a change occurs, it masks the names of users associated with those arrangements by including only their first name and the initial of their last name, and then updates these names in the database..

Notice how it correctly inferred the use of both Firebase (AngularFire2) and RxJS.

I then asked ChatGPT about the significance of masking the name. Its response was spot on perfect.

What do you believe the significance of the masked name might be?

The masked name format, where the last name is replaced with an initial, is often used as a way to protect user privacy. By showing only the first name and the initial of the last name, it provides a level of anonymity while still allowing users to be distinguished from one another.

In a system like this, which appears to involve hymn arrangements, it could be that users are contributing or commenting on arrangements, and their identities need to be partially obscured to protect their privacy, while still providing some level of personal identification.

It's also possible that this is a stylistic choice, and the system prefers to present user names in this format. However, without more context, these are just educated guesses..

This was a straightforward, almost trivial example. I chose it because it was easy to follow. That said, this technique is particularly useful if you are trying to determine not only what unfamiliar code does, but also why.

Generating Code from Data

Another cool use I have found for ChatGPT is that you can paste some data you get from a web service (or similar) response and ask the AI to convert it into a different data format, or even code that will represent that data's shape.

For example, let's say you have some sample data that looks like this:

```
{
  "contacts": [
    {
      "id": "1",
      "firstName": "John",
      "lastName": "Doe",
```

```
  "email": "johndoe@gmail.com",
  "address": {
    "street": "123 Main St.",
    "city": "Anytown",
    "state": "CA",
    "zip": "12345"
  },
  "phones": [
    {
      "type": "home",
      "number": "555-555-5555"
    },
    {
      "type": "work",
      "number": "555-555-5556"
    },
    {
      "type": "mobile",
      "number": "555-555-5557"
    }
  ]
 }
]
}
```

You can ask ChatGPT to provide you with an interface

or a class in the language of your choice. Here is the TypeScript interface it provided:

> Provide an interface in Typescript that would represent this structure
>
> Here's how you might define a TypeScript interface to represent the structure of the JSON object you provided:
>
> ```
> interface Contact {
>   id: string;
>   firstName: string;
>   lastName: string;
>   email: string;
>   address: Address;
>   phones: Phone[];
> }
> interface Address {
>   street: string;
>   city: string;
>   state: string;
>   zip: string;
> }
> interface Phone {
>   type: string;
>   number: string;
> }
> interface ContactsList {
>   contacts: Contact[];
> ```

> }
>
> In these interfaces:
>
> - `Contact` represents an individual contact with properties for id, first name, last name, email, address, and an array of phones.
>
> - `Address` represents the address of a contact.
>
> - `Phone` represents a phone number of a contact, including the type of phone (home, work, mobile) and the phone number itself.
>
> - `ContactsList` represents an array of `Contact` objects, matching the top-level structure of your JSON.

I've been favoring JavaScript and TypeScript throughout the book, but just to show that it can and will do more, I asked it to generate a Python object from that data. It gave me this:

> Generate a Python object from that same data
>
> In Python, you can represent structured data using dictionaries, lists, and primitive types like string, integer, etc. Here's how the provided JSON structure could be represented as a Python object:
>
> ```
> contacts = {
>   "contacts": [
>     {
>       "id": "1",
>       "firstName": "John",
>       "lastName": "Doe",
>       "email": "johndoe@gmail.com",
>       "address": {
> ```

```
      "street": "123 Main St.",
      "city": "Anytown",
      "state": "CA",
      "zip": "12345"
    },
    "phones": [
      {
        "type": "home",
        "number": "555-555-5555"
      },
      {
        "type": "work",
        "number": "555-555-5556"
      },
      {
        "type": "mobile",
        "number": "555-555-5557"
      }
    ]
  }
]
}
```

This Python object `contacts` has the same structure as the JSON object you provided. In Python, the equivalent of a JSON object is a dictionary (dict), an array is a list, and string, number, and boolean values are represented as str,

> int/float, and bool respectively. The keys of the dict are the property names from the JSON object, and the values are the corresponding property values, which can be other dicts, lists, or primitive types.

To be honest, I don't know Python, so I can only guess as to its accuracy, but it looks convincing.

Programming Language Translation

Another area where ChatGPT excels is translating code from one language to another. Let's say I am trying to reuse some code from an Angular Service in a React application I'm building. I want to translate the code from a TypeScript class to pure JavaScript.

It's a modest class but will serve as a fine example. Asking ChatGPT to translate it into functional JavaScript yields the following code.

We won't dive into the `MersenneTwister`, other than mention that it's an algorithm for generating random numbers. That's a topic for another day.

> Given the following TypeScript class, provide me functional JavaScript I can use in its place.
>
> export class ShuffleService {
>
>   random: MersenneTwister = new MersenneTwister();
>
>   seed(slug = 'xyz'): void {
>   const hash = this.hashCode(slug);
>   this.random.seed = hash;
>   }
>
>   hashCode(str: string): number {

```
    return Array.from(str)
      // eslint-disable-next-line no-bitwise
      .reduce((s, c) => Math.imul(31, s) + c.charCodeAt(0) | 0, 0);
  }

  shuffle(array): any[] {
    return this.random.shuffle(array);
  }
}
```

This is what it came up with.

Here's how you could represent the provided TypeScript class as a functional JavaScript object, using JavaScript's prototypical inheritance:

```
// Assuming MersenneTwister is available in the scope.
function ShuffleService() {
  this.random = new MersenneTwister();
}
ShuffleService.prototype.seed = function(slug) {
  slug = slug || 'xyz'; // default value
  const hash = this.hashCode(slug);
  this.random.seed = hash;
};
ShuffleService.prototype.hashCode = function(str) {
  return Array.from(str)
    .reduce((s, c) => Math.imul(31, s) + c.charCodeAt(0) | 0, 0);
};
```

```javascript
ShuffleService.prototype.shuffle = function(array) {
  return this.random.shuffle(array);
};
// Usage:
// const shuffleService = new ShuffleService();
// shuffleService.seed('abc');
// const shuffled = shuffleService.shuffle([1, 2, 3, 4, 5]);
```

In this JavaScript version, the `ShuffleService` function acts as a constructor for the ShuffleService object, and methods are added to the object's prototype. This way, all instances of ShuffleService share the same methods, which is more memory efficient. It's a common pattern for creating "classes" in JavaScript.

Please note that in the `seed` function, we're using JavaScript's `||` operator to provide a default value for `slug`. If `slug` is not provided or is falsy (e.g., `null`, `undefined`, `""`, `0`, `NaN`, `false`), it will default to `'xyz'`.

Remember, TypeScript is a superset of JavaScript, so all valid JavaScript is also valid TypeScript. TypeScript mainly adds static types, classes, and other features to make JavaScript more manageable for large-scale projects.

Framework Translation

It can also help rewrite code from one framework into another. Continuing the example from above, I have a small Ionic-Angular component that I want to reuse in my Ionic-React application. I can simply copy and paste that code and have the new framework code given to me.

Original Ionic-Angular Component

```
<ion-card>
  <ion-card-content>
    <div class="symbols symbols-{{card?.length}}">
      <div class="symbol-wrapper"
       ngFor="let cardSymbol of card">
        <div class="symbol"
         appRandomRotation>
          <div appThrottledClick
           [class]="cardSymbol"
           (throttledClick)="onSymbolClick(cardSymbol)"
           [throttleTime]="2000">
            {{cardSymbol}}</div>
        </div>
      </div>
    </div>
  </ion-card-content>
</ion-card>
```

Ionic-React Component from ChatGPT

Rewrite the above Ionic-Angular Component in Ionic-React

Here's an equivalent example in Ionic-React. Keep in mind that React is quite different from Angular, so there's no direct one-to-one mapping of all concepts. In React, we don't have decorators like `@Output()`, instead we use props to pass functions and data around.

```
import React, { useEffect, useState } from 'react';
```

```
import { IonCard, IonCardContent } from '@ionic/react';
import _ from 'lodash';
function SymbolComponent({ cardSymbol, onSymbolClick }) {
  const handleClick = _.throttle(() => {
    onSymbolClick(cardSymbol);
  }, 2000);
  useEffect(() => {
    // Include your appRandomRotation logic here.
  }, []);
  return (
    <div className="symbol-wrapper">
      <div className="symbol">
        <div
          className={cardSymbol}
          onClick={handleClick}
        >
          {cardSymbol}
        </div>
      </div>
    </div>
  );
}
function CardComponent({ card, onSymbolClick }) {
  return (
    <IonCard>
```

```
      <IonCardContent>
        <div className={`symbols symbols-${card?.length}`}>
          {card?.map((cardSymbol, index) => (
            <SymbolComponent
              key={index}
              cardSymbol={cardSymbol}
              onSymbolClick={onSymbolClick}
            />
          ))}
        </div>
      </IonCardContent>
    </IonCard>
  );
}

export default CardComponent;
```

In this code:

- `CardComponent` is the main component that corresponds to your Angular template. It receives a `card` prop (which should be an array), and a `onSymbolClick` prop (which should be a function).

- For each symbol in `card`, it renders a `SymbolComponent`.

- `SymbolComponent` receives a `cardSymbol` and the `onSymbolClick` function as props.

- Clicking on the symbol will trigger the `handleClick` function, which throttles the `onSymbolClick` function so it can't be called more frequently than every 2000ms. For throttling, we're using the `throttle` function from lodash.

- The \`appRandomRotation\` logic isn't included because it's not clear from your Angular code what it does. You should replace the comment in the \`useEffect\` hook with the appropriate logic.

Please note that this is a basic translation from Angular to React. There may be additional optimizations or best practices that could be applied depending on the specifics of your application..

Notice that it recognized the need to extract the Angular `appRandomRotation` directive and let me know that they would need to be created separately. It didn't do that automatically, simply because I didn't provide it with the directives' code.

Amazingly, it correctly inferred the functionality of my `throttledClick` directive and wrote its own version for me! Where was this level of sophistication when I was trying to get it to write my unit tests?

Angular Material Component from ChatGPT

Maybe I don't want to use Ionic at all but want to stick with Angular and use the Angular Material components instead. I asked it to convert the same code to Angular Material and got this.

Rewrite that Ionic-Angular component again, but this time keep Angular, but convert the components to Angular Material.

Angular Material is a UI component library for Angular that provides a set of pre-built Material Design components. Here is your Ionic-Angular code translated to use Angular Material components:

```
<mat-card>
```

```html
<mat-card-content>
  <div class="symbols symbols-{{card?.length}}">
    <div class="symbol-wrapper"
      *ngFor="let cardSymbol of card">
      <div class="symbol"
        appRandomRotation>
        <div appThrottledClick
          [class]="cardSymbol"
          (throttledClick)="onSymbolClick(cardSymbol)"
          [throttleTime]="2000">
          {{cardSymbol}}</div>
      </div>
    </div>
  </div>
</mat-card-content>
</mat-card>
```

In this code, the `ion-card` and `ion-card-content` components are replaced with `mat-card` and `mat-card-content` from Angular Material, respectively. Other parts of the code remain the same.

Please note that in order to use Angular Material components, you'll need to import the `MatCardModule` from `@angular/material/card` into the module that declares your component.

Remember, Angular Material does not provide an exact equivalent for every Ionic component, so some adjustments might be necessary depending on the specifics of your application.

ChatGPT correctly recognized that I can continue to use my Angular directives as-is.

I hope you see how powerful it is to be able to experiment (and even learn) multiple frameworks this way.

Release Notes

ChatGPT can help you generate your software release notes. This one is relatively new for me, and it took me a while to figure out what works best. I tried to start with actual diffs, but ChatGPT doesn't like long passages of text. Instead, I decided to use git commit messages. Here is a sample from an actual project of mine:

Add photo (#23)

    Added capacitor and capacitor storage

    Converted student service to promises?

    Fixed DeleteStudent, but not perfectly

    Removed RxJS from storage service

    Student CRUD working

    Added some more functionality

    Refactored some of the storage code

    Added New Student functionality

    Added camera feature

    Standardize state management within the student service (#22)

        refactor: add explicit modifiers to service signatures

        refactor: simplify syntax in student service

fix: initialize service with stored data

refactor: move state changes into student service

refactor: use routerLinkActive to determine link state

chore: format all files with prettier

chore: prefer single quote for strings

Added camera feature

Made some minor tweaks for the workshop

Minor tweaks for conference

I asked ChatGPT to group and prioritize this list into release notes.

Given the following string of commit messages for a pull request, generate some release notes, grouped by common themes and sorted by perceived importance. <I pasted the messages here>

Release Notes

This release introduces significant improvements to our application, focusing on enhancing functionalities, introducing new features, and streamlining our codebase.

New Features

1. Added Photo Functionality (#23): This update introduces photo capturing capabilities, further enhancing the user experience.

2. Added New Student Functionality: Users can now add new students through the application, improving the application's overall functionality.

3. Added Capacitor and Capacitor Storage: We've introduced capacitor storage for better data management and persistence.

Enhancements

1. Enhanced Student CRUD Operations: Made several improvements to Create, Read, Update, Delete (CRUD) operations for students, making these operations more robust.

2. More Functionality Added: Additional functionalities have been included in this update to increase the versatility of our application.

3. Camera Feature Enhancements: Made improvements to the camera feature to ensure better usability and performance.

Refactoring and Code Quality

1. Student Service Conversion to Promises: We've refactored the student service to use promises for better asynchronous handling.

2. State Management Standardization within Student Service (#22): Standardized the state management within the student service to ensure a more consistent approach.

3. Refactored Storage Code: Improved the storage code for better readability and maintainability.

4. Code Formatting with Prettier: Formatted all files using Prettier to ensure a consistent coding style across the application.

5. Service Signature Modifications: Added explicit modifiers to service signatures for increased clarity and code quality.

6. Simplified Syntax in Student Service: Refactored the student service to use simpler syntax, improving readability and maintainability.

7. Moved State Changes into Student Service: Consolidated state changes within the student service to simplify state management.

Fixes

1. Fixed DeleteStudent Operation: Resolved issues with the

> DeleteStudent operation, though some minor issues may still exist.
>
> 2. Service Initialization with Stored Data: Fixed an issue where the service wasn't initializing with stored data correctly.
>
> ## Miscellaneous
>
> 1. Minor Tweaks for Workshop and Conference: Made minor adjustments to the application in preparation for a workshop and conference.
>
> Thank you for your continued support, and we look forward to bringing more improvements and features in our future releases!

I can honestly say that it did a much better job than GPT 3.5 did the first time I tried it. I would be comfortable committing that to the git repository with my code. In fact, did you notice that it generated markdown? I've been trying to edit that fact throughout most of the book but thought it would be useful to point out here. The release notes it gave me are suitable for copying directly into a RELEASE_NOTES.md file in GitHub.

Generating Function Documentation

ChatGPT can also generate documentation for your code. For the next prompt, I gave it the complete and simply asked for a JSDoc block.

```
buildDeck(numberOfCards: number, slug = ''): Deck {
  this.shuffleService.seed(slug);
  this.shuffledSymbols = this.shuffleService.shuffle(SYMBOLS);
  const rawCards = this.dobbleService.dobble(numberOfCards);
  const deck = rawCards.map(card =>
```

```
    this.buildCard(card));
    return this.shuffleService.shuffle(deck);
}
```

Please provide a JSDoc block for the preceding function

JSDoc is a markup language used to annotate JavaScript code, which helps with providing documentation and understanding of the code's purpose. Here is a possible JSDoc annotation for your function:

```
/*
 * Builds a deck of cards.
 *
 * This function takes a number of cards and an optional slug. It seeds the shuffle service with the slug,
 * shuffles the symbols, generates a raw set of cards, builds each card, and then shuffles the deck.
 *
 * @param {number} numberOfCards - The number of cards to generate for the deck.
 * @param {string} [slug=""] - The slug used to seed the shuffle service. Defaults to an empty string.
 *
 * @returns {Deck} The shuffled deck of cards.
 */
```

This JSDoc block provides a description of the function, its parameters, and what it returns. In the parameter descriptions, it specifies the types of the parameters and whether they are optional (using square brackets around the parameter name). The `@returns` tag describes the type and purpose of the returned value.

It does a passable job at understanding the meaning of the code and giving you a reasonably complete comment. If you need more, you can always ask it.

> Expand the JSDoc to include an example for each input parameter and wrap the comments at 60 characters for better printing.
>
> Sure, I've expanded the JSDoc with examples and wrapped the comments at 60 characters for better printing.

```
/
* Builds a deck of cards.
*
* This function takes a number of cards and an optional slug. It
* seeds the shuffle service with the slug, shuffles the symbols,
* generates a raw set of cards, builds each card, and then
* shuffles the deck.
*
* @param {number} numberOfCards - The number of cards to generate
* for the deck.
* Example: 52
*
* @param {string} [slug=''] - The slug used to seed the shuffle
* service. Defaults to an empty string.
* Example: 'my-seed'
*
* @returns {Deck} The shuffled deck of cards.
```

> */
> The examples should give developers an idea of what type of input the function is expecting, which is especially helpful when dealing with less common types or formats.

Important, Non-Development Tasks

As a software developer, your responsibilities extend beyond just writing code. AI-powered tools like ChatGPT can support a myriad of non-development tasks to enhance your productivity, communication, learning, and even add a bit of fun to your day. Whether it's brainstorming ideas, summarizing documents, preparing for presentations, or even practicing mock interviews, ChatGPT can offer assistance. Here's a list of some other tasks where ChatGPT can be your go-to partner.

Brainstorming

With ChatGPT, brainstorming can become a more structured and prolific process. Whether you need fresh ideas for a new project or solutions for an existing challenge, ChatGPT can generate a diverse set of possibilities. It's like having a brainstorming partner available 24/7, providing you with an array of ideas and perspectives.

Code Reviews

Code reviews are a crucial part of software development, and ChatGPT can help make them more effective. It can assist in crafting clear, concise, and constructive feedback, which will help your peers improve their coding skills and produce better code.

For one of my code reviews, I provided a short list

of what I thought needed to be improved in the code. ChatGPT rewrote it in a much more pleasant style, even extrapolating and explaining *why* the code should be changed.

Learning New Concepts

Learning new concepts, especially in technology, can be daunting. As we have seen, ChatGPT can describe code in plain English. Likewise, it can help by breaking down complex, non-coding topics into simpler, easy-to-understand explanations. It's like having a tutor who's always available to answer your questions.

Document Summarization

Going through lengthy documents can be time-consuming. ChatGPT can help summarize these documents, providing you with key points and saving you valuable time. Whether it's a technical paper, a lengthy email thread, or meeting minutes, ChatGPT can distill the most critical information.

I was approached by a book publisher who wants to translate one of my books into Korean and sell it in Korea. ChatGPT was able to create a list of bullet points of everything in their translation agreement and offered a few suggestions where it might be improved to my benefit.

Writing Assistance

Whether you're drafting a technical blog post, writing a report, or creating software documentation, ChatGPT can assist you. It can help structure your thoughts, suggest better phrasing, and ensure your content is clear and concise, saving you time and effort.

I often have ChatGPT rewrite my emails to sound more professional, or more personal, or sometimes even less obnoxious.

Preparing for Presentations or Meetings

ChatGPT can help you prepare for meetings or presentations by generating talking points, anticipating questions, and formulating responses. It's like having a personal coach that helps you build confidence and deliver impactful presentations. An interesting exercise is to paste in the text of an article and ask it to break the article into talking points and to describe the slide for each one. Combining that with the new AI features of PowerPoint will help you create a killer presentation.

Language Translation

Need a quick translation of a phrase or sentence? ChatGPT can provide you with instant translations for various languages, aiding in smooth cross-cultural communication and understanding.

Mock Interviews

Preparing for a job interview? ChatGPT can act as a mock interviewer, posing both technical and behavioral questions. It helps you practice your responses, boosting your confidence for the actual interview.

Mental Breaks

Everyone needs a break! ChatGPT can engage you in a light-hearted conversation, tell you a joke, or share interesting facts. It's a great way to relax and recharge during a busy day.

As you can see, ChatGPT can be an invaluable companion to software developers and professionals in various fields, offering assistance, boosting productivity, and enhancing communication, learning, and organization.

THE FUTURE OF SOFTWARE DEVELOPMENT

Image by NoName_13 from Pixabay

Is this the end of software development? Is it time to panic? Should we all pack up our laptops and learn a trade? I don't think so, no. Things will certainly change, but in my experience, these types of changes are usually positive things overall.

AI tools and technologies are having a significant impact on the field of software development. However, I don't believe that they will completely replace software developers in the near future.

As we have seen throughout this book, AI can certainly automate some aspects of software development, such as code generation, testing, and debugging. AI can also assist in the design process, as you saw earlier in the chapter on project management.

Eventually, I believe these tools will be able to help developers analyze code, predict bugs, and provide recommendations for improvements.

Software development is a complex and creative process that involves much more than just writing code. It requires domain knowledge, problem-solving skills, and an understanding of the users' needs. It's not just writing code, but also testing, deployment, maintenance, and updates. AI can certainly help with some of these aspects, but it cannot replace human intelligence and creativity.

In fact, as AI becomes more prevalent in software development, it is likely to create new opportunities and areas for growth. Developers will need to learn how to work with AI tools, understand their limitations, and use them effectively to enhance their own skills and productivity.

While AI will undoubtedly play a significant role in the future of software development, it is unlikely to completely replace the need for human developers. Rather, AI will complement and augment their skills, leading to more efficient and effective software development.

Should You Be Worried?

Should junior developers and people just starting out

worry that an AI will take their jobs? Again, I believe the answer is no.

If you are a new, junior level developer or someone who is just starting out in software development, you should not be overly concerned about AI taking your job.

Think of AI like power tools for software development. Just as power tools are designed to make a carpenter's job easier and more efficient, AI tools are designed to make a developer's job easier and more efficient. Power tools allow carpenters to work more quickly, accurately, and safely, and AI tools provide developers with similar benefits.

However, just as power tools don't replace the need for skilled carpenters, AI tools do not replace the need for skilled developers. Both carpenters and developers need to have a deep understanding of their craft, including the underlying principles, best practices, and techniques. They also need to have problem-solving skills and creativity to find new and innovative solutions to the challenges they encounter.

Furthermore, just as power tools require maintenance and upkeep to function properly, AI tools require ongoing development and improvement to stay relevant and effective. Developers need to stay up to date with the latest advancements in AI technology, learn how to use these tools effectively, and adapt their skills as needed.

With the right training, attitude, and mindset, you can build a rewarding and fulfilling career for yourself in software development.

I think we'll look back on this time as one of exciting growth and opportunity. Eventually we'll wonder how we ever got along without these tools.

Amazon Review

If you enjoyed this book, I'd appreciate you leaving me a positive review on Amazon, which you can do here: https://www.amazon.com/review/create-review?asin=B0C56TTL2V

Bonus Materials

If you haven't already done so, please don't forget to sign up for the book's bonus materials at https://walkingriver.gumroad.com/l/pair-programming-bonus

---

Those who sign up for my bonus materials will also be eligible for occasional sneak peeks and discounts on future books and other content.

Updates and Questions

And remember, if you have questions or just want to be updated about this and future books, feel free to sign up at the link above, or send an email to michael@walkingriver.com.

I'm also very active on Twitter, where you can find me posting as @WalkingRiver.

And now, I urge you to go forth

and create cool things.

BOOKS BY THIS AUTHOR

Don't Say That At Work

Don't Say That at Work is an essential read for anyone looking to enhance their communication abilities and sidestep potentially expensive errors. The author, a seasoned software developer with nearly three decades of real-world experience, delves into the communication challenges we all encounter and offers a unique take on the power of persuasion. Through real-life examples and practical guidance, this book equips you with the tools to communicate effectively in any setting.

Get it here: https://amzn.to/3ObI3OI

How To Deploy Any Web Application To The Apple App Store: Make Your Application Available To Millions Of Ios Users In About An Hour With Ionic's Capacitor

If you are a web developer and want to build mobile apps, but you do not want to take the time to learn multiple technologies, then this book is for you.

These days, you don't have to ignore standard Web technology such as HTML, JavaScript, and TypeScript.

I will show you not only how easy it is to build your own app, but also how fun it can be. You will see how you can quickly take your existing Web application and deploy it to the Apple App Store and make it available to millions of iOS devices.

Did you know that almost a third of all apps in the Apple App Store are built with Web technologies? How amazing is that? Now it is your turn. Get your favorite Web app ready and join me on this fast-paced journey to enter the world of mobile application development.

Get it here: https://amzn.to/42BnfVa

PAIR PROGRAMMING

The "Pair Programming" series is a comprehensive exploration into the synergistic world of software development and artificial intelligence. The series guides readers through innovative methods of using AI to enhance traditional programming practices, starting with GitHub Copilot in the first book, and moving onto the advanced capabilities of OpenAI's ChatGPT-4 in the second. Through real-world examples, practical techniques, and insightful strategies, the series illuminates how AI can transform coding workflows, boost productivity, and drive innovation, catering to both seasoned developers and newcomers alike. This series is more than just a technical guide - it's a roadmap into the exciting, rapidly evolving future of software development.

P-Ai-R Programming: How AI Tools Like Github Copilot And Chatgpt Can Radically Transform Your Development Workflow

Discover the future of software development with P-AI-R Programming: How AI Tools like GitHub Copilot and ChatGPT Can Radically Transform Your Development Workflow. This comprehensive guide offers invaluable insights and practical examples to help you harness the full potential of AI-assisted pair programming, regardless of your experience level.

Embark on an exciting journey as we delve into the world of AI and learn how to elevate your programming skills with cutting-edge technologies.

Get it here: https://amzn.to/3o11nUj

Pair Programming With Chatgpt

Pair Programming with ChatGPT: AI-Enhanced Coding for the Modern Developer is a book that explores the exciting world of using artificial intelligence and machine learning tools to assist in software development.

One of the key themes of the book is the role that AI can play as your pair programming partner, and how it can enhance the process of writing code. I explore specific ways that AI can be used to help with complex algorithms, coding styles, and unit tests, considering both the potential benefits and challenges of using AI in these areas.

Get it here: https://amzn.to/42VxUtC

ABOUT THE AUTHOR

Michael D. Callaghan

With over 25 years of professional software development experience, Michael Callaghan has carved out a reputation as a provider of top-tier solutions across a spectrum of industries. His passion for programming, ignited in high school, led to a fulfilling career that commenced in earnest in 1995. Beyond his technical prowess, Michael is known for his in-depth understanding of the tech industry's complexities. His books, available on Amazon, address the impact of poor communication on software projects and are considered essential resources in the field. Michael's insights have guided many organizations in avoiding costly errors and enhancing their communication quality. A respected authority in software development, Michael's commitment to sharing his expertise is unwavering.

Printed in Great Britain
by Amazon